Praise for *Finding Allies, Building Alliances*

"Given their remarkable success as leaders in both business and government, Mike Leavitt and Rich McKeown have written the ultimate how-to on collaborative leading in business, government, and virtually any organization. In these transformational times, when organizational challenges have never been greater, bringing and keeping people together has never been more critical. The eight elements described in *Finding Allies, Building Alliances* create a playbook for success for every reader. I couldn't recommend it more highly."

—**Senator Tom Daschle,** former U.S. Senate majority leader

"I observed firsthand Mike Leavitt's skill at bringing people together and building coalitions in government, politics, and international affairs. *Finding Allies, Building Alliances* explains how successful managers cooperate to achieve goals and get things done in an environment brimming with complexity, uncertainty, and a multiplicity of actors."

—**Robert B. Zoellick,** former president of the World Bank Group,
U.S. Deputy Secretary of State, U.S. Trade Representative

"I've had the opportunity to work with Mike Leavitt and Rich McKeown and see firsthand their skills as problem solvers that made them so effective at finding solutions on the ground in China. Through vivid examples here, he lays out how to get individuals with seemingly competing interests to work together towards solving a shared problem."

—**Henry M. Paulson Jr.,** chairman, the Paulson Institute, and former secretary,
U.S. Department of Treasury

"In our increasingly interconnected world, organizations face a growing number of challenges—disruptive technologies, regulatory reform, environmental issues—they cannot tackle in isolation. In *Finding Allies, Building Alliances,* Leavitt and McKeown advocate for formal, process-driven collaborations between organizations facing collective problems, explicitly designed to achieve an outcome with value for each of them. Great collaborations cannot be undertaken casually—they require effort, leadership, structure, process, and commitment. *Finding Allies, Building Alliances* offers a unique and practical approach to co-opetition in the 21st century."

—**Craig Mundie,** senior advisor to the CEO, Microsoft Corporation

"In *Finding Allies, Building Alliances,* Leavitt and McKeown lay out practical steps any leader can follow to convene collaborators, gain consensus, and craft lasting solutions. Here is the recipe for any organization to solve problems more efficiently."

—**Harvey V. Fineberg,** MD, PhD, president, Institute of Medicine

FINDING Allies, BUILDING Alliances

8 ELEMENTS THAT BRING— AND KEEP—PEOPLE TOGETHER

Mike Leavitt

Rich McKeown

JB JOSSEY-BASS™

A Wiley Brand

Jacket design by Adrian Morgan

Published by Jossey-Bass
A Wiley Brand
One Montgomery Street, Suite 1200, San Francisco, CA 94104-4594—www.josseybass.com

Jossey-Bass books and products are available through most bookstores. To contact Jossey-Bass directly call our Customer Care Department within the U.S. at 800-956-7739, outside the U.S. at 317-572-3986, or fax 317-572-4002.

Wiley publishes in a variety of print and electronic formats and by print-on-demand. Some material included with standard print versions of this book may not be included in e-books or in print-on-demand. If this book refers to media such as a CD or DVD that is not included in the version you purchased, you may download this material at **http://booksupport.wiley.com**. For more information about Wiley products, **visit www.wiley.com**.

Library of Congress Cataloging-in-Publication Data

Leavitt, Mike (Mike Okerlund), 1951-
    Finding allies, building alliances : 8 elements that bring—and keep—people together / Mike Leavitt, Rich McKeown. —First edition.
    pages cm
    Includes bibliographical references and index.
    ISBN 978-1-118-24792-1 (hardback); ISBN 978-1-118-28587-9 (ebk);
    ISBN 978-1-118-28247-2 (ebk)
       1. Strategic alliances (Business)   2. Business networks.   I. McKeown, Rich, 1946-
II. Title.
    HD69.S8L42 2013
    658'.046—dc23

            2013020325

Printed in the United States of America
FIRST EDITION
HB Printing   10 9 8 7 6 5 4 3 2

To our collaboratively inspired spouses,
Jackie Leavitt and Barb McKeown,
who have endured and even enjoyed
our adventures in public and private service.

CONTENTS

FOREWORD

A THEORY ABOUT ALLIANCES AND PARTNERSHIPS

by Clayton M. Christensen

Each faculty member in my group at the Harvard Business School is invited annually to summarize his or her current research to the other members of the group. I titled my talk last year "*We ain't discovering new ideas.*" To explain this to my colleagues, I created a spreadsheet that covered the huge whiteboard that covered the front of the room. In the top row on the left-most column I wrote *Level of analysis*. Then below it in that column I labeled the rows, in sequence, *nations, industries, corporations, business units, teams*, and then *individuals*. I explained that the lowest level—individuals—was nested within teams, which was nested within business units, which was nested in corporations, and so on. Then in the top cell of each column, I labeled the column by a prominent problem that bedevils managers. In the top of the second column, for example, I wrote, *Why leaders fail;* I labeled the next column *How people and organizations learn;* the next was *How culture is created;* and so on across the board. With this spreadsheet as an organizational mechanism, my colleagues and I began to fill in, as best we could, the dominant theory or research that academia had developed for each cell.

For example, in the column of *Why leaders fail* and the row of *nations*, we wrote the thesis of Paul Kennedy (Yale) in his magnificent book *The Rise and Fall of the Great Powers*. In the next row, labeled *industries*, we summarized the work of Carroll and Hannan (Cornell) as organizational evolution. In the next row—*corporations*—we penned in my own (Harvard) theory of disruptive innovation. And in *business units*, we summarized the theory of Robert Burgelman (Stanford)—inter-organizational ecology— and so on. Each of the scholars we listed had developed a theory at a specific level of analysis about why leaders fail. When we finished that column and stepped back to review what we had written, however, we realized that the different theories at the level of nations, industries, corporations, business units, teams, and individuals actually were the same fundamental idea. Because academia is organized by the rows in the spreadsheet, each of us had inadvertently discovered the same theory. Each had conveyed the idea with unique language so we each received tenure at our respective universities. But it truly was one theory in that column, not six.

Our group then tackled the topic in the next column, which was *How people and organizations learn*, by summarizing the dominant paradigm at the level of nations, industries, and so on. And when we stepped back to admire our work in that column, we saw the same pattern: it was the same basic idea from top to bottom—just articulated in a language unique to the communities of scholars at each level. We then worked through the remaining columns and saw the pattern over and over again.

As academic explorers we each felt like Columbus when we discovered a new world, only to confess later that there already were people living there. Hence, the name of my presentation: "*We ain't discovering new ideas.*"

The only time in which this didn't occur was in the column labeled *Effective alliances*. We struggled to identify compelling theories about effective alliances at *any* level of analysis. We recorded: "We sure hope that somebody—someone who is *really* smart—tackles this issue in a compelling way."

Then a remarkable thing happened. A year later I received a book draft without a cover whose first chapter was titled "The Collaborative

Foundation: What It Is and Why It's Essential Today." When I perused the early pages I learned that it was written by Mike Leavitt and his former chief of staff, Rich McKeown. Although I had admired Governor and then Secretary Leavitt from afar, I steeled myself against what I expected to find when I read the draft—yet another vacuous autobiography by a politician whose career had ended too early.

I was stunned by what I found when I read this book, however. Mike Leavitt wasn't your average politician, of course. But Mike isn't your average scholar, either. In terms of the matrix I described above, he and Rich have given us a theory of alliances that is as insightful at the level of nations as it is amongst individual people. His theory helps us understand the past—such as why the Articles of Confederation could not work—and why the current U.S. Constitution does. But his theory clarifies the present, too, such as why Surescripts allows bitter enemies to work together without ire.

One of the most difficult tasks we confront is to learn the right things from our own experiences. When we succeed at a difficult task, too many of us learn that the hammer that worked once is the tool to be used in every situation. In contrast, Secretary Leavitt, in forging alliances as different as cleaning air at the Grand Canyon, creating Western Governors University, and facilitating agreements on how insurance companies will record health care data in a standard format, followed very different paths. His theory is contingent-specific. Leavitt and McKeown articulate the different situations you might find yourself in, and then tell you the path you need to follow to be successful in each. The book is filled with if-then statements.

What I love the most about this book is that it exudes Mike Leavitt's humility. In every chapter, in every negotiation, in every achievement, and in every lesson learned, the focus isn't what Governor or Secretary Leavitt *did* but on what he *learned* that will help the rest of mankind succeed, too. This book is truly a rare gift. I often wish people good luck as they start a project. But you don't need luck to absorb this book. It is a delight. On behalf of all of your readers, I say thanks!

INTRODUCTION

Ensign Peak is a mountain summit that rises behind the state capitol building in Utah. Early settlers climbed it because it afforded them a view of the entire valley. During my time as governor, I often climbed Ensign Peak at lunch for exercise. At the summit, I would imagine the barren landscape the settlers beheld and contrast it with what I saw—a matrix of highways, utility systems, businesses, schools, hospitals, and neighborhoods.

The social landscape shows a similar growth in variety and complexity. To bring order to the complex sociology, politics, and economic self-interest of any growing society, government was established. Centuries ago, it was the best mechanism anyone had to organize society and get things done, but over time, governments have shown that they can be cumbersome, slow, and inefficient. Many other large organizations have similar drawbacks. Today, competing global economies engage in contests to produce the best value—the best product or service at the lowest cost. Speed to market is essential, as is innovative problem solving.

The old models—huge, bureaucratic, and singular—are increasingly disadvantaged, as they are unable to provide the value, speed, and innovation people need. Collaborative alliances or networks, however, can do so. I've led and participated in dozens of networks, and I've seen how the best of them open new frontiers of productivity. Perhaps even more important, they're able to solve challenging problems that single entities cannot crack. A diverse alliance, well led and well managed, can bring resources to bear on a problem that no organization can match—even the largest of organizations. The synergy of resources— from financial to intellectual—can deal effectively with a wide range of issues confounding organizations today.

I know all this is true because I've lived it. My own experiences and those of my coauthor, Rich McKeown, have taught me just how critical value alliances are to *enacting* change effectively. I was elected governor of Utah three times, serving nearly eleven years, and then held two Cabinet posts—as head of the U.S. Environmental Protection Agency and secretary of the U.S. Department of Health and Human Services (HHS)—both under President George W. Bush. Prior to my public service, I was CEO of the Leavitt Group, now the nation's third-largest privately held insurance brokerage. After my political career ended, Rich and I organized a health care intelligence business that advises large health care organizations on managing the uncertainties of a rapidly changing marketplace. In all these endeavors, both within and outside government service, identifying organizations with aligned interests and building collaborative alliances has been critical to success. These alliances helped us organize the 2002 Olympics in Salt Lake City when I was governor. They also played a key role when I was HHS head and worked with governments and businesses throughout the world to improve health care and product safety. In this book, I draw upon these experiences and many others to share why I'm so passionate about the power of alliances.

While much of this book is written in the first person as a matter of style, it really is a joint enterprise between Rich and myself. Rich is an educator, a lawyer, and a mediator; he was my chief of staff in the governor's office and when I was in the Cabinet, and he is now my business partner. He possesses the collaborative skills that are at the heart of this book. His insights will be found on every page.

Over the years, I have witnessed and participated in extraordinary collaborative efforts where members of opposing political ideologies worked together effectively, as well as other collaborations between fierce business competitors, regulatory agencies and organizations being regulated, communist countries and democracies, and conservationists and energy companies. I discovered that collaboration among allies is more than a cooperative attitude—it is skill set you can improve when you understand how to organize and manage the various participants in an alliance or network. The ability to get things done with collaborative networks is the next evolution in human productivity. Those who develop these skills will prosper in the next quarter-century. Those who don't will fall behind.

No matter how big a company might be or how many resources a single government agency might possess, a collaborative network will beat it every time. Admittedly, collaboration can be frustrating and a bit messy. However, it's often the only hope when searching for workable solutions to complex problems.

Technology makes collaboration feasible, connecting diverse organizations and individuals around the world. The Internet and other high-speed communication tools allow networks to operate efficiently in ways that were unthinkable a few decades ago. The sociology of collaboration, though, is the tricky part of the equation. Connecting people, unlike connecting networks, is much more art than science. Assembling a diverse group of individuals and organizations, facilitating their work together, and sustaining it long enough to get the job done is an ambitious goal—but it is a more achievable goal if eight key elements are present.

During our years running governments, businesses, and political organizations, Rich and I have led or participated in hundreds of collaborative networks. Many achieved their ambitious goals, but others did not. We organized a study of why some succeeded and what caused others to fail. That effort validated our intuition that these eight key elements are required for a collaborative network to succeed:

- *A common pain:* A shared problem that motivates people and groups to work together in ways that could otherwise seem counterintuitive.
- *A convener of stature:* A respected and influential presence who can bring people to the table and when necessary keep them there.
- *Representatives of substance:* A group of collaborative participants who bring the right mix of experience and expertise for legitimacy, along with the authority to make decisions.
- *Committed leaders:* Individuals who possess the skill, creativity, dedication, and tenacity to move an alliance forward even when it hits the inevitable rough patches.
- *A clearly defined purpose:* A driving idea that keeps people on task rather than being sidetracked by complexity, ambiguity, and other alternatives or distractions.
- *A formal charter:* A set of established rules that create stability and help resolve differences and avoid stalemates.
- *The northbound train:* An intuitive confidence that an alliance will get to its destination and achieve something of unique value, and that those who aren't on board will be disadvantaged.
- *A common information base:* A shared pool of information that keeps everyone in the loop and avoids divisive secrets and opaqueness.

This book explores each element in depth, discussing why it matters and how to integrate it into an alliance. In addition, you'll find stories illustrating each element, most drawn from my experiences with various alliances, networks, and other collaborative groups. While a few of the stories will be adjusted to protect the privacy of the parties involved, many provide the names of the organizations and the individuals who guided them. The collaborations featured here run the gamut from large, ongoing global alliances to smaller networks designed to solve a short-term problem.

For instance, one collaborative group is called Surescripts, formed between two bitter business rivals—each representing a competing segment of their industry—that decided to work together to create an electronic prescription highway. Another is GEOSS, a global coalition that provides its members (companies, countries, and the like) with information from scientific observation stations throughout the world to deal effectively with changes on the planet. A third is the Remote Sales Tax Commission, a collaboration involving businesses, government representatives, and others trying to find solutions to the inequity and lost state revenue that result from untaxed Internet sales.

In all these stories of high-level alliances, the eight elements of collaboration were crucial to success. With the eight elements—discussed in Chapters Two through Nine—I hope to provide the inspiration and the information you need to be a better collaborator. Whether you intend to convene a collaborative group or increase the effectiveness of one you've joined, this book will help. It will also help you decide which networks to join and which to avoid. It provides a field-tested process you can apply to just about any type of collaborative group, helping it create lasting solutions quickly and effectively.

Chapter Twelve makes the argument that the capacity to find well-aligned collaborators and build value-creating alliances can be a marketplace differentiator for both countries and enterprises, and that a well-organized free market economy increases this capacity. In a global economy, the present and especially the future belong to the best collaborators, not the biggest organizations or the ones with the best resources.

Creating or joining a value alliance should be every leader's goal. To achieve this goal, though, you need to understand what a value alliance is and how it can confer competitive advantage on its members, so that is the topic of Chapter One.

ONE

The Collaborative Foundation
What It Is and Why It's Essential Today

Any organization seeking to increase the efficiency of its problem-solving efforts needs to understand the foundational concept of a value alliance. At its root, a *value alliance* is a group of participants with aligned interests pursuing an outcome with value for each of them. However, it is not an ad hoc or informal effort, not the sort of casual cooperation people engage in every day as they pursue their mutual interests in work, social, and governmental arenas. Instead, a value alliance is a formally organized entity following a process that has been deliberately designed to achieve a collective advantage. In such an alliance, the pursuit of *value* is the purpose and *alliance* is the platform. Collaboration is the means.

While value alliances can be formed in pursuit of joint opportunity, they most often coalesce in response to a complex but common problem. Various entities share a certain pain—for instance, businesses in the same industry struggling with a larger common issue such as the changing marketplace or an environmental concern—and they collaborate in order to diminish or eliminate this pain. We've found that problems provide a stronger impetus to collaborate than opportunities and are usually the catalyst for value alliances. That isn't to say, though, that value alliances fail to capitalize on opportunities. Quite the contrary—the solution to a complex problem often produces an opportunity.

Value alliances begin by addressing scary-looking problems—problems so overwhelming that it's difficult to see the opportunity that exists when you look to solve them. Once groups get past the initial challenge of dealing with the tough issues, though, they begin to realize that they're not just eliminating a negative, they're also capitalizing on a positive. In collaborative terms, this simply means that when organizations come together to solve a complex problem, they may well discover that it is an opportunity in disguise.

For instance, when Bank of America created one of the first credit cards in the 1950s, it encountered a range of unanticipated problems, including a 22 percent delinquent rate on the cards that it had distributed widely and randomly throughout California. It spawned a new form of consumer, and fraud was also rampant. In an effort to clean up this problem and to broaden the base, Bank of America licensed its card to banks in other states—then organized an entity to deal collaboratively with the problems the banks now had in common. In essence, they formed a value alliance. This banking network eventually took over ownership of the card from Bank of America, leading to the formation of Visa in the 1970s. Initially, Bank of America thought it was creating a solution to a thorny business problem. The solution, though, produced an opportunity for one of greatest twentieth-century businesses.[1]

Value alliances can have any time frame. They may be temporary creations, existing only until they solve their complex problem. In other instances, they may raise awareness of ongoing problems and opportunities and give rise to a new collaborative group that becomes an *alliance enterprise*—a collaboration that is sustainable over the long term.

As governor of Utah, I was involved in a temporary value alliance designed to solve the problem of air pollution over the Grand Canyon. In the early 1990s, Congress was about to impose measures aimed at preventing activities that contributed to the problem in states surrounding the canyon. The governors of the states viewed many of the federal solutions as highly problematic. Congress was persuaded to allow stakeholders in the Grand Canyon region time to develop a plan to clean the air with less costly solutions. Six states, numerous tribal nations, and assorted environmental groups, businesses, and municipalities all had vested economic interests. They came together to form the Grand Canyon Interstate Air Transport Commission to collaboratively develop the plan. Though the task took more than five years, when the plan was complete, the collaboration turned to the Western Regional Air Partnership to implement the Commission's recommendations. Congress adopted the plan. States' economies were disrupted far less than might have been the case without a collaborative solution. Best of all, the air over the Grand Canyon is cleaner as a result of this alliance.

Most value alliances begin as unincorporated entities. Those that take on a longer-term mission are normally incorporated so they can exist as free-standing enterprises. Generally the value proposition comes from the enterprise's capacity to provide greater flexibility, larger economies of scale, or superior adaptability.

For centuries, farmers have formed cooperatives to solve a locally shared problem of insufficient economies of scale. Now, enabled by digital technology and the Internet, global enterprises create similar entities to achieve the same goal. In the first decade of the twenty-first century, financially strapped airlines survived by creating value alliances under which competitors share systems and equipment in order to lower operating costs. Hospitals and their suppliers have formed group purchasing organizations to achieve greater efficiency in procurement. Even nations often use value alliance–like configurations. The European Union is a union of member states that traces its origins back to the 1950s and evolved with the accession of new states as they each decided they could compete better as a network in a global economy than as independent entities.[2] The North Atlantic Treaty Organization (NATO) is a permanent value alliance where nations collaboratively align their defense assets.[3]

While technology facilitates the formation of many value alliances, sociology—the study of how people develop, organize, and work together—explains why they stay together and function at a high level.

You can put together a state-of-the-art electronic system for exchanging information among collaborators, but as effective as this system may be at channeling data, it will fail if people don't connect with each other as efficiently and productively. Over many years, Rich and I have studied how people interact in collaborative frameworks, and we've learned that it's crucial to manage the human element. Good technology rarely makes up for bad sociology in a value alliance.

Value alliances require that participants subordinate their egos, their agendas, their preferred styles, and their biases—not to mention their organizational agendas—in favor of a shared benefit. This isn't easy, especially for people who are accustomed to doing business a certain way. Perhaps more significantly, collaborating is especially difficult for competitors. People facing difficult common problems often start out with noble ambition and good fellowship, willing to make sacrifices to overcome obstacles or capitalize on a significant opportunity. But when they're under stress, when deadlines loom, when they become frustrated, when it seems as if one group is being favored over another, human nature takes over and collaborative opportunities degenerate into a tournament of self-interest.

You can dramatically increase the likelihood of success by constructing the proper framework for your alliance and employing a set of tools that minimize relationship problems. In collaboration, getting the structure and people issues right makes a huge difference. It's all about managing the human factor. If you fail to do that, the innate personal and organizational differences among collaborators will prove too divisive for the union to hold.

In a world connected by a digitized cloud, invitations to participate in value alliances arrive constantly. They may start as a small group of colleagues from different functional groups, teams, or offices using a threaded e-mail discussion to work out a problem. Frequently, competitors may orchestrate a carefully negotiated meeting to address a common threat to their profitability or their industry's future.

All collaborative efforts involve risk. They require the allocation of time, money, and people, and they may not provide a return on that investment in the short term. Likewise, they may not provide as much of a return or the type of return participants expected, or they may fail to provide a return at all. Investing time, money, and people on the wrong collaboration can be wasteful and devastating. It can cause organizations to believe (erroneously) that they must go it alone, since partnering with others has proven to be a disaster. Value alliances, on the other hand, minimize the investment risk and maximize the return by creating scale and shared investment and opportunity.

BITTER COMPETITORS, RESPECTFUL COLLABORATORS

The problems facing organizations today are complex and significant. Western businesses want to compete globally yet are stymied by the nuances of operating in markets such as China, South America, and India. Organizations see the great promise of social media to create increased customer loyalty, yet can't quite figure out how to translate this promise into profits. New technologies produce tremendous excitement across industries, yet taking advantage of these technologies cost-effectively can be a daunting proposition.

It turns out that even bitter competitors can work together and achieve a goal that benefits all participants. The story of Surescripts illustrates how a value alliance can provide a collaborative framework to solve complex problems effectively.

This story begins with a World Health Organization report stating that the United States spent more on health care per capita ($7,146), and more on health care as percentage of GDP (15.2 percent), than any other nation in 2008, without correspondingly high results.[4] The U.S. system was poorly coordinated in large part because a shockingly high percentage of medical records remained as paper files. In 2005 (as HHS secretary), I resolved to attack one of the biggest barriers to solving that problem, the variety of ways electronic medical record systems transferred information. Chief executives of three large hospitals located in the same city told me about the large investments they had made to implement electronic medical record systems. Each had purchased systems from a different vendor, and none of their systems had the capacity to share information with the others—they lacked *interoperability*. The same situation applied throughout the United States; medical record systems were not just economically inefficient, they were a factor in poor patient care. With almost two hundred different vendors developing and selling new electronic medical record systems, this problem was only going to worsen until standards relating to interoperability were created. Many medical record vendors resisted the idea of standards, whether they created them or the government did.

Something had to be done to deal with this huge problem. Creating a value alliance became the solution.

To get two hundred competitors to the table as serious collaborators, I needed some leverage. As HHS secretary I was responsible for Medicare, the largest payer of health care claims in the United States. President George W. Bush had issued an Executive Order in 2004 establishing a national goal of interoperable health information standards in place by 2014. I arranged for a second Executive Order to be issued, giving me as secretary of HHS the authority needed to organize a grand collaboration (a value alliance) around the task of creating health information standards. The Executive Order specified that the alliance would be called the American Health Information Community (AHIC).[5] To give this effort convening power, the order made it clear that Medicare would eventually begin to penalize doctors and hospitals who did not use electronic medical records that had been certified by an approved accreditation body. It was this provision that truly gained the attention of the entire health information technology industry and caused all the parties to come to the table.

I chose to chair the effort personally—this was unusual for a Cabinet officer but I thought it critical to give the effort sufficient stature. Nearly every significant technology vendor joined the alliance, great progress was made in establishing electronic medical record standards, and AHIC's efforts set the stage for another value alliance to form, this time in the private sector.

This was a massive undertaking, and I decided our best opportunity for early success was to standardize electronic drug prescriptions. Increasing the percentage of electronic drug prescriptions would save billions of dollars as well as numerous lives (doctors' sometimes illegible handwriting, misread by pharmacists, results in thousands of illnesses and deaths).

During that time, two separate groups launched collaborative efforts to build the electronic highway necessary to join pharmacies, doctors, insurers, and patients. One group consisted of pharmacies—from small independents to large chains. The other group involved pharmacy benefit managers (PBMs)—organizations hired by insurance companies and employers to manage drug costs, allowing them to aggregate the power of many insurance companies and giving them clout with drug makers.

Internally, each collaborative effort had problems. The large pharmaceutical chains and the smaller independents had always been fierce competitors and viewed each other with suspicion. The PBM organizations, too, had intense rivalries. Nonetheless, both groups were able to overcome their reluctance to collaborate with competitors because they recognized the importance of e-prescriptions for the future of their businesses.

The PBM group formed RxHub, while the pharmacy group formed Surescripts. Each was only a piece of the electronic medical record puzzle, lacking the capacity to connect with all the key players. Nonetheless, each continued to invest millions of dollars to create its separate electronic network. Over time, RxHub and Surescripts realized that their investments weren't paying off because they lacked a critical mass of traffic.

Combining the two networks may seem obvious in hindsight, but at the time, a major obstacle stood in the way of that merger: the PBMs and the pharmacies disliked each other. In fact, *dislike* might be an understatement. Pharmacies viewed PBMs as commoditizers of their business; they felt that the PBMs wanted to convince people to buy on price alone and forgo the personal relationship between pharmacists and customers. PBMs, on the other hand, saw pharmacies as roadblocks to electronic progress and savings for consumers—they felt the pharmacies were clinging to an old and inefficient paradigm. As a result, the animosity between the two groups ran deep, and many observers of the industry couldn't imagine them ever pooling their resources.

Fortunately, John Driscoll, the chairman of RxHub, and Bruce Roberts, the head of Surescripts, shared a vision of the tremendous social and economic value a combined enterprise would create. They recognized that if the electronic routing of prescriptions could become cheaper, smoother, and more seamlessly connected, it could be both a profitable endeavor and a benefit to consumers. The two of them discussed and negotiated the complicated relationships that had emerged from their combative history. It took them a year, but these two executives used their remarkable diplomatic skills to bring the two organizations together under the Surescripts name in 2008.

Though the technological challenge of combining networks was complex, getting the relationships right was just as challenging. To this day, Surescripts board members are fierce competitors in the marketplace. For instance, two of the PBMs proposed a merger that a pharmacy group saw as a serious threat to its business competitiveness. As a result, this group opposed the PBM merger and took out ads in major newspapers, challenging the propriety of the deal and the motives of its sponsors. It also filed litigation and hired lobbyists to derail the merger with legislation. Yet during this squabble, leaders of both groups served on the Board of Directors of Surescripts, collaboratively leading the value alliance and working toward solving a common problem. Their ability to do so was made possible by the skillful alignment and discipline this value alliance provided.

The new Surescripts electronic network has greatly increased the number of prescriptions flowing through the system, creating sustainability for the network. This combined entity produced savings value to consumers as well as to all the participating entities. Interoperability was achieved.

The increased use of electronic prescriptions has boosted *adherence*—the percentage of people taking their prescribed drugs—resulting in better health for patients and fewer hospitalizations. In addition, Surescripts has provided a model for converting paper medical records to electronic ones, a social benefit of incalculable value.

Five key traits were critical for Surescripts to become a value alliance—five traits that exist in every value alliance. Collaborative efforts often lack one or more of these traits, and their absence hampers the group's effectiveness from its inception. Therefore, before embarking on any formal collaboration, make sure these traits are in place:

- *Multiple interests.* In this instance, the PBMs and the retailers formed two distinct sets of interests and within each of these groups other factions existed. While multiple interests can create tension in a value alliance, they also produce creative conflict along with a range of resources and perspectives.
- *Self-interest.* Altruism is wonderful, but self-interest is what drives participants to work long and hard and with multiple parties to come up with solutions. In this instance, the participants' self-interest was completing the electronic highway for prescriptions for the increased profit of their respective members.
- *An incremental surrender of independence.* Both the pharmaceutical group and the PBMs were willing to make the mental leap from being independent to being mutually dependent. This was no small leap, given their animosity. Yet from a psychological perspective, such a surrender is necessary or participants will engage in power politics that will destroy the alliance.
- *A free-standing governance process.* Neither the PBMs nor the pharmacies run the value alliance. Instead, the executives operate with no strings attached (to their other companies). The executive committee makes decisions on its own and not in consultation with the participants' other employers.
- *Value that continues.* It doesn't matter whether the value alliance is temporary or permanent. Its benefits are ongoing. If it solves one

problem, the value of that solution continues long after the value alliance dissolves. And permanent value alliances provide a series of solutions year after year.

THE VALUE OF A VALUE ALLIANCE TODAY

Since the 1990s, the world has experienced a confluence of new economic forces. The Internet allows instantaneous global communication. Dramatic improvements in shipping technology and capacity make it possible to move goods efficiently and inexpensively from region to region. The emerging economic models of countries like China, India, Malaysia, Vietnam, and Brazil have caused dramatic increases in global competition. In most industrialized nations, too, consumption has been fueled by deficit spending. Nations and states along with individual families and businesses have taken on piles of debt and now face limits on new borrowing and spending.

In this environment, people and organizations no longer have the luxury of inefficiency. No one can afford to operate slowly or at a financial disadvantage globally. With these new financial parameters, efficiency has become a matter of survival. As the economy evolves, value alliance–building will become a Darwinian determination of who survives.

That's because networks are simply more efficient than non-networks. As many businesses have learned, networks trump silos just about every time. It no longer matters how big a silo is. Networks offer the advantages of speed, diverse resources, flexibility, and connectivity that singular entities can't match. Even some of the largest airlines, retailers, and online marketers have formed networks of competitors, suppliers, vendors, and others to deal with issues that are too challenging to manage on their own. Just as networks of smaller computers have proven superior to mainframes, a network of varied organizations is far more efficient than a large, slow-moving company. Singularity is inherently inefficient.

The problems facing organizations today have become so complex that it's unrealistic to expect any single company—even one as large and dynamic as General Electric, Wal-Mart, or IBM—to solve them on its own. When affected parties collaboratively gang up on complex problems, value alliances produce superior results for at least four reasons:

- *Multiple perspectives provide a more complete picture of a problem, creating more options, synergies, and solutions.* Even when organizations sincerely solicit diverse ideas and opinions, they can only take these efforts so far. They're limited by dominant cultures—"the way we have always done things around here"—as well as by an employee population that to a lesser or greater extent has been trained and developed with the company's and industry's existing perspectives in mind. Value alliances bring together participants that are much more diverse in their thinking than the employees of any one organization.

- *Trust produces efficiency.* When people trust one another, business arrangements and innovative solutions can be achieved quickly. For example, Lloyd's of London is not an insurance company—it is a collaborative membership organization where people who want to share risk can come to find those willing to assume risk. Because only participants willing to abide by time-honored traditions of collaborative behavior are permitted to be members of Lloyd's, trust develops and members begin depending on one another's expertise.

- *Shared investment and reduced litigation help limit financial risk.* Looking back at the economic downturn, which commenced in 2008, many organizations are wary of any program or project that seems risky legally or financially. Leaders are highly sensitive to criticism that they squandered funds on a bad bet or to the negative publicity that results from litigation. Value alliances spread the risk of investment among participants and make it manageable.

- *Speed improves when agreed-upon standards reduce friction.* By bringing together diverse influencers from private and public sectors, value alliances can establish standards that accelerate virtually any process. With standards in place, organizations can transact business with greater ease. Sectors with well-defined standards, such as the automated teller machine (ATM) networks, allow for broader services as well as consumer ease. Bank customers with ATM cards can obtain cash from their bank accounts anywhere in the world, regardless of what bank owns the machine.

A TRADITION AS OLD AS THE UNITED STATES

While the term *value alliance* may be new, there is little new about competitors competing aggressively at one level and cooperating at another. I first heard the word *co-opetition* in 1992 when Ray Norda, the founder and CEO of Novell (a pioneer in the development of network software), used it to describe his company's business strategy. *Value alliance* as a concept goes back even further. In fact, the origins of the United States of America can be attributed to a value alliance. In 1787 representatives of the thirteen original states gathered in Philadelphia to solve a serious problem: their new country was floundering. A decade after the Declaration of Independence, the colonial states were still governed by the Articles of Confederation, and it wasn't working.[6] The country had a $60 million Revolutionary War debt and no taxing authority to pay it. Three states claimed what is now part of Vermont, but no courts had the authority to settle the borders. Trade disputes routinely divided states, and some states were even creating their own currency. There was a need for a mechanism to bring the states together.

Calls to create a national government were initially received poorly. A few years earlier Americans had won their independence from Great Britain with their blood, and they were not enthused about subjecting themselves to a big national government.

Delegates met in Philadelphia during the summer months of 1787 to explore solutions. What emerged is often referred to as the Miracle at Philadelphia: the Constitution of the United States. The miracle wasn't simply the document. It was the willingness of thirteen colonial states and the people who inhabited them to subject themselves voluntarily to a national government.

In reality, the Constitutional Convention was a value alliance. The colonial states, while competitors, shared the burden of their collective dysfunction. The founding fathers persuaded all but the most skeptical states to participate. The convention was not intended as an ongoing organization but rather a venue to explore remedies. However, at the conclusion of the convention's work, a solution was proposed: a jointly formed permanent enterprise—another alliance—to be called the United States of America.

The Constitutional Convention and the subsequent creation of the U.S. government shared all the defining characteristics of a value alliance: multiple interests, personal interest, self-interest, an incremental surrender of independence, a free-standing governance process, and value that continues.

VALUE ALLIANCES TAKE MANY FORMS

Organizations from every sector of society already benefit from value alliances. Whether these alliances are temporary or permanent responses to complex problems, they can involve participants from different functions, companies, industries, and countries who come together to address local, national, or global problems.

Western Governors University (WGU) illustrates the surprising way in which diverse sectors of society can come together. Between 2001 and 2010 the cost of a university education soared from 23 percent of median annual earnings to 38 percent.[7] The preceding decade had seen a similar increase. Subsidizing the cost of state universities and colleges had become increasingly difficult for state governments, leaving more and more of the price to be covered by tuition payments. Students complained that as tuitions increased, they accumulated bigger and bigger debts. Employers complained that universities produced workers ill prepared for the modern workplace, so many students found it hard to find jobs that fit their needs. And states found it increasingly difficult to find money in their budgets to support this unsustainable escalation of cost.

The pressure was building. In June 1995 I hosted a luncheon for the governors of western states in Park City, Utah. Our discussion of the issue was sparked when one of the governors noted that each year, universities and colleges were asking the state legislatures to fund more buildings to house growing student populations—a pressure that we all felt. Each building cost millions and fueled higher costs for maintenance and utilities. Given the growing imperative for more workers with college degrees, we knew the demand would continue to increase—and we knew that state budgets could not sustain building traditional campuses to provide education in the same old way.

Several of the governors had begun to see the potential of the Internet to deliver education. Others believed passionately that the education system's results would not improve until it began to measure student competency in practical skills acquired rather than class attendance and memorization of facts. At the conclusion of the private lunch it was obvious that we shared a problem and an interest in working together on it. That day we organized a collaborative process to explore how we could proceed, and a few months later we started a value alliance. We called it Western Governors University.

Governors, their higher education advisers, and selected business leaders came together to develop ways states could create new models of delivering higher education. Knowing we would need the involvement of the technology community for this idea to gain traction, I invited Eric Schmidt (who was then CEO of Novell, a Utah-based company) to advise our alliance. He and other business leaders provided invaluable expertise and emphasized the notion that higher education needed to be driven by measurable results. Ultimately we produced a set of ideas that traditional universities considered quite disruptive. We proposed that the western states form an alliance to develop Internet-based education delivery, rather than having every state university system work independently. Even more provocative was our desire to implement a system where students progressed and were measured by demonstrating competency in real-world job skills rather than through accumulation of credit hours.

The reaction of the state universities made it clear that we faced four barriers: bureaucracy, regulation, tradition, and turf. If our ideas to drive value in higher education were to be tried, it would require a new university.

We began putting together all the ingredients necessary to launch Western Governors University—a nonprofit institution that would be online and would cost students far less than traditional colleges or other existing online universities. We envisioned a university that would serve adult learners looking to earn a degree while still working full time—a free-standing, collaboratively developed enterprise to implement innovative ideas using collective strengths of many different organizations. We wanted to build a true network that would create new value.

Governor Roy Romer of Colorado and I took the lead in bringing together the disparate parties that were essential to the collaborative effort's success. We visited Silicon Valley and besides Eric Schmidt (soon to become CEO of Google), we brought on board Scott McNeely of Sun Microsystems and Eric Bienemu of 3 Com, two other highly regarded technology leaders. They contributed money, technical know-how, and computer systems, and in exchange they hoped their investment would help increase the number of software designers and other technologists their businesses needed, who were in short supply.

We held a meeting in Omaha, Nebraska, and nine governors—all wearing Western Governors University sweatshirts—launched the new virtual university, which was to be headquartered in Salt Lake City, Utah. Symbolically, rather than cut a ribbon, we clicked a computer mouse. The institution was designed to be unique in four ways. First, it would exist only on the Internet. Second, student progress would be measured by demonstrating competency through tests, projects, and other means. Rather than granting degrees when a specified number of credit hours were completed, we would give degrees when students had demonstrated competency in given subjects. The third difference: We would use the best online courses from other universities and learning resources rather than develop our own. Fourth, the well-qualified faculty of the university would mentor students one on one rather than teach them in large classes.

We recruited other states to participate, and over the next two years the number grew from the initial nine to nineteen. Each of the initial states contributed $100,000 seed money, but an equally significant contribution was providing the educational resources essential to design the course work and the technology provided by major Silicon Valley companies.

We sought and received support from Congress, which passed a statute that provided certain capacities before we were fully accredited. And we forged an agreement with the accreditation agencies. This was the toughest of our collaborative partners to get on board, but we knew WGU had to meet the highest national academic standards if the degrees WGU offered were to be accepted widely—that is, by employers, other schools, and those who offered financial aid—as having value. The dilemma was that there were no standards or criteria for accrediting a competency-based online university. For one thing, our online model didn't dovetail with the geographical accrediting regions. Since our students would use library resources from the Internet, we didn't have a brick-and-mortar library with stacks of books for the accreditation agency to count. Nonetheless, we persisted, and over time, we convinced the agencies that they had a responsibility to foster innovation in education, and that they had to create new standards that fit the new type of online university. The accreditation agencies worked with us as collaborators, and we developed rigorous criteria and then created a novel process under which four of the seven regional accreditation agencies participated.

None of this happened overnight, but it happened. Invariably, the multiple interests we brought together had a synergistic effect, applying diverse expertise to the issues we faced. Our technology partners and educators possessed the motivational self-interest to make our initial model even better. Together, we revamped the curriculum, focusing it on degrees that were especially appealing to older students who wanted to acquire marketable skills—in areas such as business, nursing, and technology. We invented a learning model where WGU faculty did not teach but mentored the students as they used the best of online courses from universities and private sources.

WGU is both disruptive and transformative. In the last decade, the model gained traction and took off. In 1997, our first year, WGU had three hundred students. By the end of 2013, it will have nearly fifty thousand. It continues to expand at 30 percent a year.[8] Recently states have begun to formally incorporate WGU into their education system. There is a WGU in Texas, Indiana, and Washington. The average age of a student is thirty-two. More than 75 percent of the students are working. By 2012, WGU prepared more math and science teachers than any other institution in the United States. It has a rapidly growing health school that will be among the nation's top trainers of nurses. The average student earns a bachelor's degree in thirty-one months at a cost less than one-third that of state universities. All of this is done on the revenues received from students; state governments provide no tax support.

Though Western Governors University is a nonprofit educational institution, nonprofit status was not essential to its success. The impulse to create a value alliance is even more powerful in the business world. Many times, value alliances hide in plain sight. You don't even realize that a network producing great value exists unless you do a little digging, as I discovered when I was at the airport. I bought a Delta ticket for a flight from JFK International Airport in New York City to Salt Lake City, Utah. It was to leave from Gate 17. However, when I got to Gate 17 the electronic marquee at the agent's desk announced an Air France flight. I glanced at my ticket, thinking maybe I had walked to the wrong gate. When I looked back at the sign, it was announcing an Alitalia Airlines flight. Once again I stared at my ticket, trying to figure out what was happening. Another glance at the ticket counter told me that a Virgin Airlines flight would be leaving from Gate 17. Finally, my Delta Air Lines flight number was posted. I walked to the terminal window, where I could see a Boeing 767 operated by Delta. Passengers ticketed on six different airlines would board the same jet.

Delta is part of a collaboration called SkyTeam Alliance, a group of twenty-seven airlines formed in 2000 as defensive move to survive after five of their competitors formed the Star Alliance, a network in which participants share aircraft, ground equipment, computer systems, and marketing dollars.[9] Star Alliance radically changed the cost structure and competitive landscape of the airline business.

Under a contractual membership agreement, airlines commit to align their operations with standard guidelines developed by the governing board of the alliance. They develop joint marketing programs, airport synergies, cargo systems, and compatible information technology systems. Over time, airline alliances have expanded their areas of cooperation. Typically work groups among members are formed. These groups collaboratively devise and maintain pathways of cooperation which produce common value to the members.

Prior to the 1997 formation of Star Alliance, airlines functioned like mainframe computers: siloed and completely independent, each bearing the full costs of its operations. After Star Alliance, most airlines operating outside a network could no longer compete. Within three years, SkyTeam and another airline alliance known as Oneworld had been formed. Nearly every airline in the world joined one of the three or faced elimination from the marketplace. Prior to the formation of SkyTeam, success depended on an airline assembling and operating all the components for itself. After SkyTeam, success depended on which network an airline joined or created. A siloed entry is disadvantaged when competing with an efficient, networked competitor.

FINDING THE RIGHT ELEMENTS

All the collaborations Rich and I explore in this book—the airline alliances, Western Governors University, and Surescripts, among others—possessed all eight elements essential for a value alliance. From committed leaders to the effect of a northbound train, incorporating these elements is the best action you can take to elevate your collaboration to the level of a value alliance. To facilitate this effort, the next eight chapters examine each element in detail, the challenges associated with integrating it into the collaboration, and how others have made the element work for their group.

Value alliances always begin with a common pain. People need to be motivated to leave their comfortable silos and work with other groups who come from different cultures, possess different philosophies, and may have different perspectives on the problem. Pain may hurt, but it's also a valuable catalyst for value alliances. Chapter Two takes a look at how this pain manifests itself and brings collaborators together.

TWO

A Common Pain

Enlightened self-interest is an underlying principle of any value alliance. When people are motivated by their own problems, they often discover that they can find solutions to them by responding to the interests of others. Value alliances, therefore, exist at the intersection of self-interest and common interest. Typically, individuals become collaborators when they discover that they cannot solve a problem on their own.

A natural component of self-interest is self-governance. Most people prefer to avoid situations where they lose the capacity to make their own decisions. They give up control willingly only in exchange for some other benefit. Thus, when they agree to collaborate with others, it's generally not because of an inherent social conscience or altruistic desire to strengthen their overall business or industry—it is because they view it as the best way to fulfill self-interest.

Relieving common pain is in everyone's self-interest. We've listed it as the first of the eight essential elements because in our experience, collaborations fail when participants lack this pain (or manage to eliminate it without anyone else's help). Collaborating with others is hard. It can be expensive. It always involves a surrender of independence. Few people are willing to place themselves in a collaborative position if they have an alternative.

Therefore, before forming, leading, or joining a value alliance, you need to ask this question:

Do the participants have sufficient reason to pay the price success will exact?

Or in our value alliance terms: *Is their common pain intense enough to cause them to collaborate?*

Common pain can take many forms, and you need to translate that pain into your terms: Is it a drop in market share? An environmental concern that affects the private and public sector? A danger that imperils an entire industry? An immediate threat (versus one off in the distance)? Does it hit you in the pocketbook or somewhere else? While a collaboration can seek to capture an opportunity, success is most likely when the motivator for an alliance is shared pain that requires mutual action to bring about relief.

COLLABORATIVE RESPONSES
TO SIGNIFICANT PAIN

The impulse to collaborate in response to pain has always existed, pain being the catalyst that helps people overcome their natural distrust of outsiders. The representatives at the Constitutional Convention in Philadelphia in 1787 didn't refer to their collaboration as a value alliance, but they certainly would have acknowledged the common pain of dealing with their disorganized public life.

This common pain manifested itself in various ways, but they all related to problems of union. For instance, the lack of a central authority to regulate interstate commerce created border conflicts, monetary discrepancies, and credit problems. Each of the thirteen states acted as if it were its own independent country in matters such as interstate commerce rather than part of a united country. George Washington wrote, "thirteen sovereignties . . . pulling against each other, and all tugging at the [federal] head, will soon bring ruin on the whole."[1]

Contrary to what many people believe today, none of the states were in favor of forming a union. Back then, each was fiercely independent and its leaders by and large represented the interests of its own citizens much more than the interests of the country. And yet, these leaders were hurting. Without agreed-upon standards, the states were operating inefficiently and running into conflicts with each other. This pain was financially significant, and it no doubt also undercut people's time, energy, and relationships with each other.

More than two hundred years later, in 2002, a new aviation company produced a jet called the Eclipse that seemed ideal for business use—it was lightweight, economical, and mass-produced. It was priced well below its closest competitor.[2] Many businesses, including one operated by my brothers, bought or put down deposits for Eclipses. Prior to the introduction of this aircraft, private jets were available only to the wealthiest people. While a certain level of income was obviously necessary to purchase the Eclipse, its relatively lower price point expanded the market. For this reason, a variety of individuals made major investments in the company. NASA and the FAA enthusiastically supported Eclipse as part of their collaborative vision of air taxis providing cost-effective transformation for various enterprise executives.

Unfortunately, the Eclipse soon experienced problems, including engine and other aeronautical concerns. Parts and servicing issues arose. The company went bankrupt. As a result, there was a lot of shared pain—among the owners of Eclipses, the investors, and the federal agencies that supported an air taxi concept. While some of these groups responded as individuals—filing lawsuits or eating their losses and moving on, looking elsewhere for solutions to their air travel requirements—many of them responded with a collaborative effort: the Eclipse Owners Club. They had numerous questions and concerns, and they realized that pooling their resources was the best way of addressing these issues. The business executives, pilots, investors, and others who came together to found the club were able to do so because of the Internet—technology is a great facilitator of collaboration in response to pain.

The Eclipse Owners Club has proven to be a great resource for members with concerns about the aircraft they did purchase (especially for parts and servicing) as well as about the future of the company post-bankruptcy.[3] Many members had a vested interest in seeing the company get back on its feet, not only because they had a financial stake but also because the plane provided an essential transportation tool. Without a supporting organization, owners had to jury-rig every repair and search for parts and technical expertise. They hoped the Eclipse would still prove valuable, saving time and money and increasing scheduling flexibility. To protect their investment, these owners needed a system to support their objectives. Eventually, the company emerged from bankruptcy with new owners, and the club has proven to be a great communication tool for members and prospective owners. The Eclipse Owners Club website is the main component of this communication hub, giving members access to information, events, and other resources.

Global Healthcare Exchange (GHX) is a collaboration of competing health care manufacturers (Abbott Labs, Baxter, Medtronic, and others) that created an automated network to facilitate and standardize information in the hospital supply chain.[4] Prior to the GHX collaboration in 2006, hospitals were using a nightmarish mishmash of electronic and paper systems to reach health care service and product vendors. When intermediaries emerged around 2000 and began charging a toll for their services, Jeff Immelt of GE Healthcare and other leaders in the industry perceived a third-party threat to their relationship with customers (hospitals) that could increase costs for everyone involved. These competitors responded not just to existing common pain but anticipated pain—they foresaw losing control of the supply chain process and facing additional expenses created by third-party exchanges. For this reason, these intense competitors came together and created their own industry-based exchange, investing millions of dollars and setting up a management team to run it.

When I led the U.S. Environmental Protection Agency from 2003 to 2005, the United States helped form the coalition of countries and companies we named the Global Earth Observation System of Systems (GEOSS). We realized that a wide range of governments and private organizations needed data about the weather, ocean currents, earth surface temperatures, pollution migration, and more. While the entities each sought similar information, their reasons varied widely. Some wanted to improve their ability to forecast the weather. Others saw this information as critical to anticipating the spread of communicable disease. Shipping and military organizations saw the transformative power of the data for managing their ocean fleets and airlines. Farm organizations recognized how the data could facilitate crop management.

The potential participants were in various stages of attempting to gather this data. Many nations had satellite systems and others had ocean buoy systems. In addition, there were weather monitor systems, observation reports from ship and airline pilots, and temperature sensors. The problem—or more to the point, the common pain—was that everyone had small pieces of the data puzzle but lacked the means to put the whole picture together.

I represented the United States at a meeting in Japan of more than a hundred nations to discuss organizing a collaborative solution. Representatives of nations who were at best economic competitors and at worst sworn enemies managed to overcome their competitive instincts and animosity to create a value alliance. How were they able to do it? Because each possessed self-interest in finding a way to ease or eliminate their common pain.

They came together when they recognized that no single organization or country could provide adequate monitoring of changes going on around the world. They recognized that without a good monitoring system, they were making bad decisions—countries weren't doing what they should to protect the environment, for instance, and companies were failing to recognize when product resources were diminishing. The pain was caused by lack of information, and so GEOSS attempted to diminish the pain by plugging all its members into a common information base fed by monitoring systems throughout the world. As a result, GEOSS is composed of countries and companies big and small who all feel the pain of not having sufficient information in this area.[5]

Common pain takes different forms, from intense and immediate to generalized and long term. It can motivate warring political parties to pass hotly contested legislation and resolve difficult negotiations. In fact, even the anticipation of shared pain (rather than the reality) can stimulate effective collaboration.

My mother used this technique to resolve disputes among her six sons so regularly we called it "Mother's Rules." For instance, she would employ her rules when two of us engaged in animated discussions about who would get the last piece of dessert. She would say, "We'll split the piece." If I cut the pie, my brother would get first choice. I would cut the final piece in half with scalpel-like precision, anticipating the pain of my brother taking the larger piece if I did not divide it fairly.

Whether the pain is anticipated or present, though, it is absolutely essential for a value alliance. It provides the motivation for participants to overcome their reluctance to partner with competitors or other individuals and organizations with whom they feel they have little in common.

THREE TYPES OF MOTIVATION

Common pain drives people to create collaborative groups for three different reasons:

- *Fear.* The calculation or feeling that the odds are too high that something unacceptable will take place. In the Western Governors University example, what the governors feared was that the cost of education for people in their states was rising too rapidly; that the educational opportunities being offered often didn't fit the vocational needs of their residents; that they would be unable to provide a good education for a significant percentage of their citizens in the future. Fear is the source of most common pain.
- *Greed.* The calculation that people will make more by collaborating with others than by going it alone. When numerous airlines formed the SkyTeam alliance, some of them were operating with an unsustainable financial strategy and collaborated out of fear. Others, however, saw

the alliance as a way to create short-term profits and long-term survival. For them, greed was the primary motivation.

• *Touch the hand of greatness.* We use this phrase figuratively to suggest that people are motivated by being part of noble and influential undertakings. If a value alliance is likely to help participants and their organizations achieve a high-profile success, people are motivated to be part of the process. It makes them feel good and improves their standing and that of their organizations.

In October 2007, Bill Gates convened a conference in Seattle for the purpose of organizing a collaboration to eradicate malaria. I attended as the representative of the U.S. government, the world's single largest donor to the cause. The group that assembled from around the world was a who's who in global health. Health ministers flew in from Africa. European scientists came. Asian business titans arrived. Officials of multilateral global health organizations made time on their schedule.

Eradicating malaria is a noble objective. However, somewhere in the world every day someone is holding a conference on the subject. What made people want to attend this meeting was the possibility that something quite remarkable could happen because Bill Gates was the sponsor. If nothing else, it was motivating for a health minister in Africa to be part of an effort sponsored by a branded figure as big as Bill Gates. Being a member of the collaboration formed at that meeting in Seattle made the attendees each (if only in their own minds) a little more important. Doing so allowed each of them to "touch the hand of greatness."

All three of these factors may be active in the formation of any value alliance—but fear is the primary catalyst. What we humans fear most is the loss of what we have. When change occurs—as it is occurring with greater speed and intensity in every area of work and life—we become anxious. In the business world, for instance, little motivation exists to form a value alliance when profits are high and the status quo seems likely to maintain itself. When change strikes, however, leaders feel a motivating and intuitive anxiety about growing problems or missed opportunities.

CAN YOU DESCRIBE YOUR PAIN ON A SCALE OF 1 TO 5?

Pain is a matter of perception. As a result, it can be difficult to measure. When you go to the doctor's office, you'll often find a pain chart numbered 1 to 10 with corresponding pain descriptions for each number, and it's designed to help patients communicate "how much it hurts" to their doctors. You may also be aware of the Schmidt Sting Pain Index, created by entomologist Jason O. Schmidt to measure the pain intensity from a range of stinging insects.[6] The lowest pain on his scale is 1.0 from a sweat bee sting and Schmidt dubs it "Light, ephemeral, almost fruity. A tiny spark has singed a single hair on your arm." The highest pain on the scale, 4.0 plus, comes from a bullet ant, whose sting Schmidt describes as "Pure, intense, brilliant pain. Like fire-walking over flaming charcoal with a three-inch rusty nail in your heel."

To help you measure your particular pain, here is our adaptation of Schmidt's index. Select the number that best describes the pain your enterprise is experiencing:

1. **Little or no worry.** A few problems but our leaders are confident that we can handle them effectively on our own.
2. **Minor concern about a trend or event.** Might affect our group's profits or our stakeholders in a negative way at some point in the future.
3. **Moderate anxiety.** No immediate danger, but in the middle term, our enterprise as well as some others in our field may be adversely affected.
4. **Major fears.** A crisis has raised the alarm that it will be difficult to maintain the status quo and we and others affected by the crisis need to find a solution or the repercussions will be serious.
5. **Constant, widespread danger.** A situation threatens to spiral out of control in the short term, and everyone in our field is affected; no one has a good solution and catastrophe looms.

Admittedly, these five measures oversimplify a given company's situation, but the list can provide a quick snapshot of how badly it hurts.

Clearly, if you are in the 4 or 5 pain category, you are strongly motivated to collaborate in order to solve your problem. But we've developed a more detailed measure of common pain, one that will incorporate additional factors into your measurement.

The Common Pain Index

Measuring the pain felt by essential collaborators is a litmus test of how committed the key parties will be to a shared effort. The more intense and widespread the pain, the more firm the commitment. We've created the Common Pain Index to help you gauge pain in your organization as well as in prospective collaborators. Assign yourself a numerical value between 1 and 10 for each of the following factors (10 being the highest pain) and then average the total:

- Significance of the problem.
- Dependence on others.
- Relative influence.

Significance of the Problem

What is the impact of the problem on an enterprise's success? Collaborations require time, money, and people. The collaborative process is more complex, slower, and messier than independent decision making. To be willing to give up a degree of independence and control, a given leader must believe the problem poses a serious threat to the enterprise. At the top level of pain, the problem threatens the enterprise in the short term—it will be out of business within the year if its people don't solve the problem effectively. It's still a significant problem, however, as long as the problem threatens the sustainability of the enterprise. If a country declares a no-drilling policy for environmental reasons, an oil company operating in that country may be able to survive and even do well in the short term, but if the ban remains in effect, it may spell doom to the organization five or ten years down the road.

A problem is also significant if it produces major financial losses or makes a negative impact on performance in other ways without threatening the organization's survival. In the Surescripts example, the PBM and pharmacy groups could both have continued to exist without collaborating, but they would have been operating at mediocre levels of performance and efficiency.

What all this boils down to is that a problem must cause significant pain for an enterprise or its people will not give up the independence and control that collaboration requires. At the same time, we should emphasize that some organizations respond to relatively insignificant problems by joining collaborative efforts, but they do so for political reasons or just to monitor what is taking place within the collaboration (which may include their competitors). When this occurs, they're participating in a collaboration in a very superficial way. As a result, the collaboration stands no chance of becoming a value alliance—it will lack the necessary energy and commitment of the participants.

Dependence on Others

A problem is not particularly painful if you believe you can solve it through your own resources. Even if the pain is significant, you are going to be reluctant to cede control to others to solve it if you are confident you can handle it on your own. But consider GEOSS. Some of the countries that are members of this collaboration have long histories of animosity toward each other. Yet they joined GEOSS because they recognized that without access to information on changes that could only be monitored through a global network, they would feel the pain of these changes intensely.

Leaders of enterprises need compelling reasons to cooperate with others. Some possibilities:

- Access to missing competencies
- Shared capital risk
- Reduced unit costs with greater volume
- Need for valuable information
- Combined volume for greater market power

Relative Influence

Influence is the trickiest factor, in that you must assess not only the importance of your own involvement to the collaboration but that of others as well. Not all collaborators are equal. If, for instance, the enterprise with the greatest resources and capacity to help solve a problem isn't interested in participating in a collaboration, then the pain will not be felt in the right place. More typically, two or three prospective collaborators hold the key to an effective sustainable outcome. If two out of the three (or all three) are willing to participate, then the common pain is sufficiently high. If they won't come to the table, then the pain level could be too low.

Score each participant on a scale of 1 to 10. A score of 8 to 10 indicates intense common pain; 4 to 7 suggests significant pain; 3 and below implies tolerable pain. Look at the scores as a whole and make a determination of whether you believe this proposed alliance passes the common pain test—and be sure to factor your own score into the mix.

Different Manifestations of Common Pain

Common pain can manifest itself in uncommon ways. Therefore, don't feel this element is absent just because the leaders of different potential collaborative enterprises are all complaining about varying aspects of a problem. If they all feel intense pain—even if that pain varies in type and perception—then the motivation is there for a value alliance.

What does have to be the same, though, is the timing. Simultaneous pain is crucial. If the pain motivates one collaborator to join this year, another next year, and a third two years from now, then a value alliance won't be created immediately. Effective collaborators don't have to feel the same type of pain, but they do need to feel it at the same time. In some instances, this doesn't occur because one or more prospective collaborators are unaware of the pain, are in denial about it, or don't believe the news that communicates the pain.

For instance, you would have thought that automobile companies and other organizations in their industry would have created value alliances years ago to create more fuel-efficient vehicles. Certainly some companies made efforts to create these vehicles, but it took a long time for all the players to get serious about this issue. Apparently, some auto company leaders didn't recognize how fast the cost of gasoline would rise; some leaders believed they could figure out solutions on their own; and some leaders convinced themselves that buyers would not be willing to buy electric or alternative-fuel cars in sufficiently profitable quantities. Over time, these leaders began to get past their denial, disbelief, and ego and feel the pain, but they didn't do so simultaneously, so value alliances did not emerge as early as they might have.

Be aware, too, that just because you feel the pain intensely doesn't mean that others will share this perception. What is highly motivating pain to one in a given moment may strike others in that moment as irritating or even moderately hurtful, but lacking that white-hot intensity that causes people to form value alliances. After Hurricane Katrina, the Charity Health Care System in Louisiana was in a shambles. It was an inefficient system that served its patients poorly, and the aftermath of the storm provided a great opportunity to replace it with a far more effective one. On behalf of the federal government, I offered to lead a formal collaboration to create a better system. Over the course of the next three years, we made a significant effort to gain agreement within the community about how to restructure the health care system. I made more than two dozen trips to Louisiana to work on this collaboration. It was a major commitment of my time and government resources. I met numerous times with each of the major players to assess their commitment, but unfortunately, I didn't read the situation correctly.

I learned an important lesson from the experience. While all the participants in this alliance told me they were willing to find a way to change the system collaboratively, not all the political leaders, health care officials, and other potential collaborators felt the same degree of pain. I failed to assess the degree of pain being felt and whether it was sufficient among all participants to align interests. While there was a huge amount of pain in Louisiana post-Katrina, it was not being felt as intensely by all involved parties. After this experience, I determined that never again would I make such a significant commitment without assessing the pain of all key participants. Using the Common Pain Index model, I would have concluded that some of the participants were not feeling the same type and degree of pain as others. Lacking sufficient common pain doomed the alliance.

THREE

A Convener of Stature

At its core, a value alliance requires a convening power: someone with the stature to bring together a group of independent parties and have them work in an aligned way to create something of value. While common pain may provide the motivation for various groups to participate in a collaboration, they still need a convener of stature to capitalize on that motivation, providing credibility and cohesion.

At some point, you've probably received an invitation to participate in a collaborative enterprise. If you didn't accept that invitation, it was probably because you didn't feel the problem the group was addressing warranted the investment of your time and resources. It may also have been, however, that you were unfamiliar with the convener; or you were familiar but didn't regard the convener as possessing sufficient influence, authority, or power to make something happen.

Earlier I referred to Bill Gates and how he served as a focus in the effort to eradicate malaria. It's difficult to imagine anyone turning down an invitation from Bill Gates to collaborate—and the inability to turn down an offer is one sign that you're dealing with a convener of stature.

WHAT MAKES A CONVENER OF STATURE?

Former President Bill Clinton is clearly a convener of stature. Consider the Clinton Health Access Initiative (CHAI), designed to provide greater access to health care in developing countries for treatment of AIDS and other diseases. Because of President Clinton's global brand—as a former U.S. president and as an individual dedicated to helping those in need around the world—he has been able to attract more than seventy partner countries and other members to CHAI's procurement consortium, which purchases AIDS medicines and diagnostic equipment at reduced prices. Becoming a partner with CHAI requires an investment of time, money, and other resources, but President Clinton is perceived as an individual of high social integrity and achievement, drawing a range of partnering countries to the table.[1]

With Surescripts, Bruce Roberts and John Driscoll were the heads of fiercely competitive groups that had each created electronic prescription highways. They became the co-conveners of stature who helped create the Surescripts value alliance. Both Bruce and John had earned tremendous respect in their field, not only from the particular groups they represented but from their competitors as well. Both men had the reputation of being straight shooters, of being open-minded, of having strong values. In fact, when Bruce and John met for the first time, they each remarked that they sensed the other's open-mindedness with regard to a collaboration—and other members of their parties sensed it as well. Looking back, they see this trait as a key factor in bringing their members into the collaborative entity. In fact, it is fair to say that they were the ideal conveners for Surescripts, in that their stellar reputations helped all parties envision the possibility of a collaborative solution to their electronic prescription problems. If other conveners of lesser stature had tried to organize a collaborative effort, prospective participants might have refused to attend the initial meetings, or attended them with a high degree of doubt and skepticism.

Former Navy Vice Admiral Conrad C. Lautenbacher was both the convener of GEOSS and its committed leader. He was also the undersecretary of Commerce for oceans and atmosphere as well as the administrator of the National Oceanic and Atmospheric Administration. With his distinguished naval service as well as a Ph.D. from Harvard (in applied mathematics) and work as a management consultant, he commanded tremendous respect in a wide variety of communities—environmental, governmental, global, military, and business. When he called the first Earth Observation Summit in 2003, he set the stage for convening GEOSS two years later. GEOSS needed a convener with a broad record of achievement. To bring together the diverse countries and companies that combined to form GEOSS, the convener had to command respect from various audiences.

Conveners of stature can have three forms:

- An individual
- An organization
- A combination of individuals and organizations

As noted, Surescripts had two individual conveners. Combinations are sometimes necessary to secure participation from a critical mass of groups that a single convener couldn't secure alone. For instance, President Clinton co-convened various efforts in Africa with the administrators of local hospital districts, because their stature had greater resonance in those remote areas.

At times, organizations are more effective conveners than individuals. A variety of organizational types—a company, a trade group, a community-based entity, a think tank—can use organizational structure and reputation to provide convening power to solve complex problems. For instance, a local PTA convenes leaders from various parts of the community to combat the growing problem of gang violence. Or a trade association convenes competitors to establish production standards that would protect its industry from bad practices.

In some instances, multiple organizations can act as conveners. A few insurance companies, two hospitals, a large medical clinic, a long-term care facility, and a local community health organization all helped convene a value alliance that established a more efficient way to manage patient care in their community.

Conveners often have positional authority. People who hold elective office can use this authority to crystallize collaborative effort. Similarly, business leaders or influential organizations often emerge as conveners of stature. What these conveners have in common is persuasiveness or prominence within a specific community. People are often attracted to good conveners because of their ability to lead and motivate or their eloquence at presenting the problem and the need for a collaborative situation. In some instances, of course, a convener possesses both positional authority and persuasiveness, and this is the best scenario of all for the collaboration.

Seven Essential Qualities

Conveners may have very different personalities and leadership styles, and may be either individuals or organizations. Nonetheless, the most effective ones share seven traits:

- Trusted brand
- Relevant reach
- Adequate independence
- Diplomatic skill
- Instinct for stage setting
- Astute perception
- Ability to apply pressure

Trusted Brand

Prospective conveners, whether individuals or organizations, come to the task with a personal brand—a reputation that defines expectations of potential participants. For successful conveners, this brand must include *fairness*—the reputation for being even-handed and honest in their dealings with employees, the community, competitors, and others.

Trade associations or nonprofit organizations often exist to serve a higher purpose than making money for themselves, thus earning the trust of people in a given sector. They possess governance structures designed to accommodate a variety of interests, allowing them to serve a moderating, conflict-resolving role that also engenders trust. The Western Governors Association (WGA) meets this criterion for a trusted brand. It is a nonprofit group that was organized to serve the shared interests of states in its region. It has bylaws that were crafted to protect against partisanship or bias toward one area or interest. When Congress looked for a convener of stature to oversee a collaborative process to clean up the air over the Grand Canyon, WGA's long history of impartiality and fairness made it a logical choice.

In some instances, an individual or an organization with a trusted brand may still be the wrong choice as a convener in a particular situation. For example, Joan (not her real name) was a university president who first recognized the need to gather elements of the educational, business, and local communities to address the growing problem of teens dropping out of school and falling into a cycle of drug use and criminal behavior that was harming the community on a number of fronts. To her credit, Joan recognized that she would not make an ideal convener of stature. Though she was highly accomplished in her field and had done a good job at the university, she came from an elite background and was seen by some members of the community as not fully understanding the needs of the less privileged in the area. Aware of this fact, Joan called on Angela, a recently retired dean at the university, to be the convener. Angela came from a background similar to the one the value alliance would address, and she had been active her entire career working with volunteer groups in the low-income areas adjacent to the university. At the same time, Angela was considered to be unbiased—she had worked well with two minority groups in the community, even though she was a member of neither minority.

Relevant Reach

Potential conveners of stature always have limits to the range of people and groups they are able to attract or influence. Aside from some world-renowned leaders, few people or organizations can issue an invitation

45

and expect all types of collaborators to respond immediately and posi-tively. When I was governor of Utah, I would often invite people who had influence in the state's political arena, business sectors, and other communities to come together and collaborate, and it was unusual for anyone to turn me down. Whether it was out of respect for the office, concern that they might miss out on an opportunity, or because they liked the prestige of meeting with the governor (and especially at the governor's mansion), they usually obliged.

On the other hand, when I would issue an invitation to collabora-tors outside my state or my sphere of influence, I was much less likely to elicit a positive response. Generally, they turned me down—not because they didn't like or respect me but because I wasn't sufficiently relevant to their goals and agendas. Conveners must seek a match between their range of influence and their universe of collaborators. Most conveners know the limit of their influence intuitively. For instance, they recognize that they will have clout with anyone in their own field nationally but that their influence is only local when it comes to government and business participants. Or they may under-stand that their influence isn't what it once was—they may have held a high position but now occupy a lesser one with correspondingly less influence.

The best conveners test the limits of their influence before they issue formal invitations to collaborate, holding one-on-one conversations with all prospective participants before issuing invitations to join. In this way, they can test the likelihood of their invitation being accepted. I remem-ber receiving a call from the chief of staff of a VIP testing the likelihood that I would accept an invitation. He explained the nature of the prob-lem they were working to solve and said his boss "would be inclined to ask you to participate, if you would be inclined to accept." While I was amused at his choice of words, it struck me that his call saved us both from a potentially awkward situation. When a call like this comes from staff and not the principal, consider it a preliminary conversation and not necessarily a lack of commitment. When the principal calls it is a true invitation. Conveners need a good sense for which prospective participants to address directly, and which will respond better to an inquiry from a staff member.

When conveners recognize intuitively or through investigation that their influence is too limited to get the value alliance going on their own, they may wish to partner with another convener (an individual or organization) to fill in the gaps in their influence. We noted earlier that with Surescripts, John and Bruce had to be co-conveners, since each of them had influence only in his respective area—each needed the other to gain full participation for the collaboration.

Participants collaborating to solve a complex problem want to know that their convener possesses a level of knowledge necessary to understand this problem. When Bill Gates and the Bill & Melinda Gates Foundation convened a summit to wipe out malaria, he and his foundation were seen as having the necessary reach because they had displayed competence in handling health care issues in the past. Sometimes, conveners are well-intentioned and sincere about wanting to solve a given problem but people see them as dilettantes. Stature isn't only about past accomplishment, title, and reputation but about a given convener's perceived knowledge about the problem at hand.

Adequate Independence

Prospective conveners are often motivated to create an alliance because they have a vested interest in the outcome. A convener's passion for an issue or a specific problem-solving approach is important, conveying the necessary level of commitment. But those who come to a collaboration with a solution that benefits their own company far more than other collaborators will not be viewed as credible. Similarly, those who are seen as being beholden to special interests or as having a reputation for favoring one group over another will lack the independent stature necessary to be effective conveners.

Diplomatic Skill

Because the main function of conveners is to bring the right parties to the table, they must be proficient in the art of diplomacy. Feuding competitors frequently must work together collaboratively. Similarly, the CEO of a large corporation may not be eager to work with the head of a consumer group that has been criticizing that company for years. Diplomacy often involves massaging egos, appealing to the greater good, and managing conflicts. Perhaps most important of all, conveners must gain contingent agreements among separate parties to join the collaborative entity and then bring them together into a functional whole. This often takes finesse that some leaders—especially leaders used to command-and-control approaches—may lack.

Instinct for Stage Setting

A sense of stage management also comes in handy for conveners in need of a dramatic demonstration of the importance of the alliance. Sometimes using a prestigious setting to make an invitation does the job—the governor's mansion served me well. Other times, however, setting the stage requires more elaborate plans. In these instances, convening a value alliance requires what I call "flags and bagpipes."

When I was head of the U.S. Environmental Protection Agency, the president asked me to build a value alliance to improve water quality in the Great Lakes. It required the involvement of six states, many local governments, several federal agencies, environmental groups, advocates, and business heads. As convener, I had spent a lot of time using my diplomatic skills to secure commitment from the most important participants. Still, I could envision some of the participants backing out of the collaboration at the first whiff of disagreement about the solution. So I decided we required a major event to cement all participants' commitment to this effort. We found a large, stately room and on the stage put a table with the flags of all the participating organizations. As the governors, mayors, captains of industry, and others entered, they were serenaded by bagpipers.

As we marched into the room, I walked next to one of the region's big city mayors whose participation was crucial. As the bagpipes sang out with their distinctive pulsing drone and the drums rolled, the moment felt tremendously meaningful. The mayor turned to me and said, "This is a really big deal, isn't it?"

Everyone signed the document pledging commitment, but more than that, everyone felt a strong sense of commitment to the goal of the enterprise. This value alliance, which became known as the Great Lakes Regional Collaboration, created a unified group now being used to keep the Great Lakes water quality improving.[2]

Astute Perception

Whether by intuition, instinct, or a learned skill conveners need to be perceptive of what motivates people to participate in an alliance of people or entities. A friend who served as CEO of a major U.S. company was concerned about how some first-world companies were exploiting workers in third-world countries. He worried workers were being paid poorly and forced to work in unsafe conditions. My friend issued an appeal for participation in an effort to create nonexploitive standards to a group of prominent companies doing business in affected countries. His general approach was to appeal to prospective participants' sense of fairness. However, as he talked with them it became evident that while they regretted the injustice, they were not motivated to take up his cause. For these my friend took another tack, asking them what they thought might happen if they did nothing and the glare of public scrutiny fell on their practices. He then answered his own question by suggesting that their brands would be diminished. He pointed out that world opinion would condemn them for exploiting these workers, so it was to their advantage to be proactive.

With a combination of approaches tailored to his audience, my friend got 100 percent participation.

Ability to Apply Pressure

The convener of a value alliance sometimes needs to skillfully apply action-motivating pressure to clarify and create the reality of the common pain strong enough to make collaboration an attractive alternative.

William (not his real name) was inaugurated as a university president during a time of great financial stress. As he looked for efficiencies, the way the university was deploying technology caught his attention. It was clear that millions of dollars could be saved by having a campus-wide IT system rather than each department having its own. As in many large organizations, however, the various departments wanted to retain the power to control their own technology.

William recognized that he had the power to impose a top-down solution, but he also knew that many deans would protest any unilateral change—no matter how good it looked to an outside observer. Instead, he decided to organize a collaborative solution by convening a value alliance. Knowing that a technology change was in the offing, some of the deans began dragging their feet, saying they had too much on their plates to join such an alliance.

William understood that sometimes a convener of stature needs to provide a sense of urgency to ensure that the group is motivated. He let it be known in a university-wide memo that the continuing economic loss caused by the various technology platforms was unsustainable and that reductions in technology might have to be made if a solution wasn't found. Second, in private discussions with various deans, William communicated that each dean's preferred choice of software and technology might well be taken away if wholesale cuts were required.

Almost immediately, the departmental technology teams and their deans felt common pain—the potential of losing their funding and their ability to design the system. They made the work of the value alliance their highest priority. As is often the case, once their collective energies were applied to finding innovation, excitement ensued. The campus technology community got a better system and William got his budget relief.

Five Responsibilities of a Convener

Convening a group of people to create value collectively is an act of leadership. Having led organizations over many years and closely observed some of the world's best-known leaders, I know that conveners must complete the following tasks:

1. Define the problem and consequences of inaction contrasted with what the value alliance aspires to accomplish.
2. Organize a structure that furnishes the alliance with people, perspectives, and an orderly method of operation.
3. Create a system of accountability.
4. Mold a culture of productivity.
5. Recognize good performance and respond to poor behavior.

First Responsibility

Define the problem and consequences of inaction contrasted with what the value alliance aspires to accomplish.

In assembling the participants of a value alliance, the convener must make a case to potential participants that the problem being undertaken by the value alliance is of sufficient urgency to justify their commitment and the associated investment in time and money. Painting a clear, compelling picture of what will happen if the value alliance doesn't do its job is just as important as communicating the positives if it succeeds.

Second Responsibility

Organize a structure that furnishes the alliance with people, perspectives, and an orderly method of operation.

Like the casting director for a play, a good convener carefully inventories the points of view that must be represented, weighs the political dynamics, and considers the mix of personalities needed to produce a credible and valuable outcome. Then it becomes the convener's job to recruit the participants, call the first meeting, and establish a form of governance and operation within the group.

Third Responsibility

Create a system of accountability.

Value alliances require a method to hold people accountable for their particular responsibilities. The convener's job is to put a system of accountability in place. Successful value alliances do eventually adopt a management structure to ensure accountability. Early on, though, this structure is just taking shape, so conveners need to take on the task of establishing time tables, receiving reports, and judging the adequacy of the work.

Fourth Responsibility
Mold a culture of productivity.

Leaders establish a culture through their personal example and interaction with others. However, the most important thing a convener does to mold the culture is to select people who have high collaborative intelligence. In addition, when there is potential for disagreement, people generally behave in a more temperate fashion when they are in the presence of a person they respect.

Fifth Responsibility
Recognize good performance and respond to poor behavior.

Experienced leaders understand the importance of rewarding good performers. Everyone needs to be appreciated and—especially since nearly all value alliances consist of people who have other jobs or are there in voluntary capacities—keeping morale high is critical. Likewise, there are times when tensions surface or people misbehave. The convener of stature can often be called upon to help handle those situations.

DRAW ON INFORMAL CONVENER EXPERIENCES

While you may have experience leading a business, political group, nonprofit organization, or some other entity, this may be your first experience acting as a convener of a value alliance. If so, think back. At some point in your past, you probably fulfilled a convener role, even though you may not have thought of it in those terms. Thinking about how you successfully convened another group—and how you solved the problems inherent in a convener role—will serve you well when you convene a value alliance.

Here are some of the most common informal convener roles:

- Organizing a committee formed by a school community to devise a new scheduling system
- Chairing a group of department heads when your business needed a recommendation for a new technology vendor
- Establishing a committee of members to develop alternative solutions to a financial problem for an organization you served as chairman of the board
- Working with vendors to develop a just-in-time inventory system for a new product your company was developing
- Assembling a group of parents to serve as the committee to develop a plan to upgrade officiating quality for a youth sports league

Leaders who have these types of experiences can often translate them to formal value alliances. In fact, they often find that all their leadership roles help prepare them for many of the requirements of convening, including helping recruit representatives of substance, as discussed in Chapter Four.

FOUR

Representatives of Substance

The top priority for conveners is identifying the right people and securing their participation in a value alliance. As one Washington D.C. society maven told us, getting the right people together was key to her success in influencing events and issues she cared about. "I like dinner parties with a purpose, and I assemble a guest list as if I were casting a play; every actor has a part," she said. It was no wonder that she was widely esteemed for her ability to assemble gatherings of people who had great influence, and that made her invitations especially welcome.

The casting analogy is apt. As noted in Chapter Three, value alliances need to be cast like plays. Finding the right ensemble of people—individuals with talents that blend well, as well as the financial backers for the play—is essential. Conveners who possess the same skills as this society maven cast their collaborations with keen instinct as well as great knowledge of potential participants.

SUBSTANCE OF THREE TYPES

We refer to participants in a value alliance as *representatives of substance*. In most cases, people are invited to represent a point of view or stakeholder interest in the discussion. *Substance* refers to the requirement that participants be sufficiently well respected that their involvement inspires confidence. As a group, they need to possess the collective influence in the marketplace of ideas to bring about a solution to a shared problem. They are not only prominent people, they are people with access to resources (financial, human, technological), and what they say and do has the power to move others. We look for participants who possess at least one and ideally all three varieties of substance: authoritative, cognitive, and reputational.

Authoritative Substance

People with authoritative substance possess the legal capacity to make or influence decisions on behalf of their organizations. For this reason, representatives of substance tend to be senior within organizations. It diminishes the viability of a collaborative process if those sitting at the table have to ask permission or consult with others before agreeing. This isn't simply a matter of expediency. When organizations send mid-level people to participate, it is often a sign they are not feeling sufficient common pain and their participation may be more monitoring activity than commitment to action.

In Chapter Two, we wrote of lessons learned from involvement in an unsuccessful effort to reform Louisiana's charity health care system after Hurricane Katrina. One of the critical participants was Louisiana State University (LSU). Without full buy-in from LSU, reform wasn't going to happen. Very early in the process, however, LSU began sending progressively lower-level people to the meetings. As convener, I was worried that LSU lacked commitment. With hindsight, I realize that I should have done more than worry. If I had addressed the issue of authoritative substance effectively, the effort might have succeeded.

Cognitive Substance

Cognitive substance involves special knowledge that is sometimes needed to understand the implications of certain alliance issues. This knowledge may include scientific understanding or a working knowledge of process; it can also be hard-won experience. Mark Twain once said, "If you hold a cat by the tail you learn things you cannot learn any other way." Having savvy veterans at the table who know which end of the cat to hold on to is invaluable.

Reputational Substance

Reputational substance suggests those for whom respect is more important than likeability or collaborative intelligence. Such representatives often hold strong views that may be controversial or unique. These participants, though, are respected—even by their competitors—for their accomplishments and ideas. This respect can cross boundaries or be limited to a given organization or industry, but reputation helps create the level of trust within the collaborative entity that is crucial during stressful periods.

Lloyd's of London was formed in 1688 in Lloyd's Coffee House. Lloyd's is a place where risk syndicates organize collaborative risk-sharing arrangements.[1] As a young businessman I developed an idea that required me to enlist the support of a number of several risk-taking syndicates. I learned that each syndicate is represented by a person known as an underwriter. This person assesses the risk presented by a particular situation and makes a decision as to whether that syndicate (a collection of people) will participate.

After a number of discussions with various Lloyd's syndicates, I had dinner with Edmund (not his real name), a well-regarded underwriter, to talk about my idea. During dinner, he asked me, "Are you familiar with the phrase *uberrimae fidei*?"

"Yes," I replied, "I know it's the motto of Lloyd's of London and that it means 'in utmost faith.'"

Edmund said, "Yes, Lloyd's of London is an organization built on trust and reputation. When I put my signature on a line slip, people follow it. They trust my judgment and my integrity. They expect me to live by the spirit and letter of the contract. At Lloyd's if you have good judgment, operate transparently, and keep utmost faith, you succeed. Break it once, and you're finished."

Edmund told me he had studied my proposal and was going to endorse it. He said, "Other syndicate leaders trust my lead, and a sufficient number of them will follow that you will have no trouble [getting enough support]."

Edmund was a representative of substance. He had tremendous knowledge of the insurance business (cognitive substance), the standing to give me the go-ahead on my plan (authoritative substance), and the respect and trust of his colleagues (reputational substance).

Recruit the Edmunds of the world to your value alliance.

A FIVE-STEP PROCESS

Physicists refer to *impetus*, meaning the force that puts things in motion. Getting the right people together provides the impetus to solve problems and to get things done.

No matter how local or global the problem your value alliance is being formed to solve, having the right participants matters. The following five-step process increases the likelihood of a successful result:

1. Define and match the task to the convener.
2. Make a list of the communities of interest.
3. Balance manageable size against inclusion.
4. Choose prospective participants with interpersonal dynamics in mind.
5. Rely on the "contingent ask" to secure participation.

Step One

Define and match the task to the convener.

The stature of the convener should match the significance of the issue the alliance is trying to resolve. When people organize to solve problems they often take on more than is feasible. Large or amorphous issues substantially reduce the likelihood of a workable match.

The stature of the convener influences this process. For instance, a convener in the oil industry who sought creation of a value alliance to deal with the diminishing volume of oil reserves throughout the world would probably find it hard to gather all the right representatives from businesses, governments, environmental groups, and so on. On the other hand, if you're a present or past president of the United States, you might have a realistic chance of success.

In 1998, I was chairman of the National Governors Association. The Internet was rapidly becoming a significant factor in the way business was conducted. It was evident that in time, online sales would seriously erode sales done in retail stores. Like other governors I welcomed and encouraged the expansion. However, I could also see changes that needed to occur with the way sales tax is collected for an online sale. In retail stores, the merchant was required to collect the sales tax on every purchase and remit it to the state. However, the way the system was structured, online merchants weren't required to collect sales tax. Such a system was unfair to brick-and-mortar retailers. Many feared that the disadvantage could in time seriously affect their ability to survive—something that has proven to be a rational concern.

As chairman of the National Governors Association, I was asked to convene a group to find a solution. Our task was to recommend to state governments a pathway forward. As you can imagine, they were dealing with an enormously complex, far-reaching tax issue involving all types of retailers as well as governments in many states.

Among the options we looked at was to seek legislation—to pass laws organizing equitable systems. However, it became evident that creating a solution would require changing laws in every state—and there was little certainty how such a process could be accomplished. The technology didn't exist and there was still great disagreement on the policy involved. We made an important decision. Our task was to develop a collaborative voluntary solution as a first step rather than trying to legislate a government response.

Step Two

Make a list of the communities of interest.

Instead of rushing to identify and invite representatives, start by determining the interests that need to be involved in solving the problem the alliance is facing. Create a prospect list by answering the following questions:

- Who will find this alliance most valuable given their organization's problems and concerns? Why?
- Given those same problems and concerns, who will find this alliance most threatening? Why?
- Who will feel the most impact from the change the alliance may catalyze?
- Who may hold a significant part of the solution to the problem facing the interested parties?
- What ideological differences are at play among prospective representatives? Who is the most articulate spokesperson for each side?
- What geographic sensitivities does the selection need to reflect?
- Are all the largest players in the list? What about other individuals who are part of smaller but significant enterprises?
- What other dominant parties can have a major influence on the outcome?
- What other groups are already attempting to solve this problem? Are there any existing ones that would be well positioned to solve it?
- What technical knowledge must the alliance have access to?

Step Three

Balance manageable size against inclusion.

There is no one perfect size for a value alliance. Typically, if the collaboration draws participants from a relatively narrow universe and the convener has hierarchical influence over them (for example, a CEO organizes a collaboration that draws from different offices within the global company, suppliers, customers, consultants), then a small group often works well. Conversely, if the collaborative entity spans industries, communities, and enterprises, then a larger group may be necessary.

Balancing the efficiency of small with the inclusiveness of large, though, is a common challenge for value alliance conveners. There is such a thing as too many representatives of substance; decision making is hampered when too many voices are trying to be heard.

How big is big enough? It varies with the specific setting and the means of communication the group will be using, but the answers to the questions in Step Two will give you a good start. Look for redundancies in substance—if two people have the same titles, represent the same constituencies, or possess the same expertise and resources, invite the one with the best fit with the group. Look for a critical mass of substance—the smallest group that contains the right mix of people to solve a problem and implement a solution.

One simple tactic is to recruit representatives whose expertise and resources satisfy multiple criteria. They may be able to provide technological support to the collaboration as well as strategic insight. In this way, you can keep the number of participants manageable.

Step Four

Choose prospective participants with interpersonal dynamics in mind.

Theoretically, everyone in a collaboration should push personal differences aside and work together to deal with the common pain. In reality, deep-rooted feuds, jealousies, and hypercompetitiveness can interfere with the collaboration. For example, Andrew was CEO of a large global corporation and Yvette was executive director of an environmental group, and tremendous animosity existed between the two (not their real names). Yvette had accused Andrew's company in public and private of being the worst contributor to waterway pollution in the region; her accusations were not just against the company but against Andrew himself, and she called him a liar and said that he had broken his promises time and again about dumping chemical products into rivers. Andrew had accused Yvette of "grandstanding for the media" and maintained that she was pursuing her own agenda rather than that of her environmental group, suggesting that she was considering a run for public office.

At the same time, Andrew and Yvette were representatives of substance; both should have been part of any collaboration attempting to set new guidelines to ease pollution of water and air in their region. The convener, though, recognized that there was too much negative history between Andrew and Yvette for that to happen. Fortunately, Andrew recognized this and stepped aside for his number two person (who had gotten along relatively well with Yvette in earlier interactions) to join the collaborative effort instead.

This is a judgment call for conveners. Creative tension fueled by competition is fine—the Surescripts experience makes that clear. When there's a lack of respect between two people, though, or when the animosity is at a high level, then other alternatives should be pursued. For instance, sometimes there's a second-in-command who can substitute as Andrew's did, and sometimes there's another organization with essentially the same expertise, resources, and mission whose top person can cover the same ground without evoking the same conflict.

Step Five

Rely on the "contingent ask" to secure participation.

When you approach people about joining your collaboration, their first question is usually, "Who else is involved?" As much as they may be motivated to collaborate to ease the common pain, they often have options for doing so—acting on their own or in another collaborative group. Therefore, to secure the participation of your targeted representatives, rely on the *contingent ask*. Introduce the concept of a value alliance to ease the pain and then provide each potential participant with a list of other likely participants in each category (business, nonprofit, consumer group, and so on). Ask them to comment on the other individuals listed—if they see them as representatives of substance. This may help you refine the list, but it also draws them into the collaboration—they are already participating by commenting. More important, though, if they are at all hesitant about joining, make their participation contingent on some or all of the other people you named joining the group. No one wants to be left out if they know that other people they respect and admire are participating.

As you discuss participation on a contingent basis, use it as an opportunity to assess the degree of productive engagement and commitment a prospect is likely to provide. It is helpful when prospects communicate concern and even some tension about serving as part of the collaboration. If people you talk to are ambivalent about their own participation or other names you provide them, then it suggests that their pain may not be intense enough to justify a value alliance. It may also indicate that they aren't sufficiently concerned about the problem to provide the energy, commitment, and resources that are required of representatives.

SECONDARY INVOLVEMENT

In many of the value alliances I have been involved in, the problems have been sufficiently intense that hundreds of people actively sought to participate. Many times, these are extraordinarily talented people who have much to offer, but keeping the size of the group manageable requires you to limit the number of participants. In such cases, we have learned to create secondary or support roles that expand opportunities to contribute and participate so as to benefit by what people outside the core group have to offer. This can be important for another reason. Omitting people from the collaboration often guarantees that they'll become external critics or even saboteurs. When people feel excluded, they often speak up against the excluders.

Conveners can create technical work groups that report back to the collaboration, allowing people outside the formal alliance a say in the outcome. It also gives the group access to what can be crucial expertise and other resources.

In the American Health Information Community (AHIC), the value alliance we created to foster data standards for electronic medical records, we had hundreds of people vying to participate. However, we wanted a small group to facilitate decision making. To apply the available talent and foster participation, we created six technical work groups that functioned as subcommittees. Two of the fourteen members of AHIC cochaired the technical work groups. The work groups were able to make recommendations to AHIC, but all final decisions were made by AHIC.[2] This tool allowed hundreds of people to be involved but kept the decision-making process manageable.

Another secondary involvement method: Designate alternates. This involves forming a group of participants who share similar backgrounds and beliefs, but only one is allowed to sit at the decision-making table of the coalition—the others may observe and participate but only one has decision-making power at any given time. This helps avoid biasing the decisions in favor of a dominant group (say, five CEOs from big chain retailers and only two ma-and-pa store representatives). Yet this method also keeps all the people actively involved in the collaboration and gives them each a turn at the table.

A number of variations on these themes can ensure secondary involvement. For instance, you can create the formal position of observer or adviser. These individuals are invited to all the meetings, allowed to submit ideas or recommendations, and may be featured prominently in the work-ups, but they aren't given decision-making authority. Similarly, you can create technical advisers for the collaboration. These individuals are called on selectively and situationally for advice, but they're not full-time members. Having technical advisers also can increase the collective substance of the collaboration.

OBSERVING THE REPRESENTATIVES IN ACTION

The final litmus test for representatives of substance is observing them in action. Sometimes, substance can be an illusion. You assume a given individual possesses expertise, then discover that you're wrong. You figure that an organization has many resources that it can lend to a collaborative effort and discover that those resources are already stretched tight. You believe a CEO or other person with position power enjoys great respect and authority, only to find that a highly abrasive personality diminishes that influence.

Observation, then, can play a critical role in reconfiguring the group you recruit for a collaboration. For this reason, holding a preliminary meeting of representatives can provide insights that will help you determine if you need to add or subtract members to achieve the right collective substance. During this initial meeting, facilitate a discussion of the problem you're forming the collaboration to address and watch for the following danger signs:

• *Naysayers.* Negativity can reduce the capacity of the group. Obviously, you want people to speak their minds and analyze proposed courses of action critically, but some individuals can be so highly critical, cynical, or pessimistic that they make it difficult if not impossible to motivate the group to take action. They make the "northbound train" (discussed in Chapter Eight) grind to a halt, focusing obsessively on worst-case scenarios and putting a damper on the group's enthusiasm. It can be in the collaboration's best interest to keep extreme naysayers out of the group—and not just because they undercut the excitement and eagerness you want participants to develop. They may turn out to be *saboteurs*—people who want the collaboration to fail—a topic addressed in more detail in Chapter Twelve.

• *Empty places.* During the discussion, it may become clear that a critical piece of the collaborative puzzle is absent. As people talk, someone may say, "We really could use someone who has strong connections with the legislatures in three key states" or "This collaboration is dependent on raising a certain amount of money and none of us seems to have access to the type of fundraising we'll require." Consensus around points like these tells you that you need to invite a given individual to join the collaboration. It may have seemed obvious from the beginning who the representatives are, but discussions of the problem often clarify the need for additions to provide the necessary collaborative substance.

• *Empty faces*. This can be a highly subjective issue, but it's worth assessing since if you have one or more collaborators who turn out not to be fully invested in the group's mission, then a value alliance won't form. Pay attention during this preliminary meeting to who speaks to the problem, and how. Is there someone who says little—or nothing at all? Is there someone who appears bored or who is just going through the motions of participating? Is the group composed of too many listeners and not enough speakers and doers? This last point is especially important, since many preliminary meetings may be marked by great discussion but little inclination or ability to take action. Great discussion often creates the impression that the collaborative group is perfectly composed. This may not be the case. While great discussion is a good sign, it can also be a misleading one. Some collaborations are all talk and no action. As noted earlier, people sometimes lack the commitment to spend the necessary time and effort to execute a solution to the problem. Therefore, observe the group for signs of commitment—for people who just don't just bandy ideas about but suggest specific courses of action that they promise to support.

A preliminary meeting has another advantage for collaborations that aspire to become value alliances: it provides an opportunity to develop esprit de corps. One of the challenges of diverse collaborations is that you're bringing together people from different and often competitive cultures and organizations. Even if they're not outright competitors, a participant may view a fellow collaborator with uncertainty. One business executive on a collaborative committee said of an executive director of a nonprofit, "His world is so different from mine he might as well work on Mars."

Conveners need to facilitate that initial meeting in every way possible: research the backgrounds of collaborators, find common ground or shared interests among members, communicate to each of them what they have in common, encourage formal and informal discussions that allow people to get to know each other, take everyone out for a meal or drinks. You want to create an atmosphere of trust, comfort, and openness as quickly as possible. In this way, you are encouraging representatives of substance to share that substance with others.

FIVE

Committed Leadership

Indecisiveness often accompanies collaborative problem solving, and value alliances need clearly designated and committed leaders who will push, pull, or cajole progress through the muddle. Keeping these alliances on track always involves conveners of stature and committed leaders—roles that may be filled by the same person but are often held by two or more. In the latter case, the interrelationship between these individuals is key. This chapter explores these roles and interrelationships, introducing you to some good committed leaders we have observed, and we offer some suggestions to help you excel as a value alliance leader.

Be aware, though, that leadership does not emerge naturally within a collaborative framework. Just because you have representatives of substance in your collaboration, that doesn't mean that any of them will take on committed leadership roles. In fact, one of two other scenarios generally occurs. In the first, no one steps up and takes charge; participants limit their involvement to attending meetings and carrying out definable tasks. In the second, most if not all representatives compete for control of the alliance. More than once I have seen senior executives jockey for control of the white board because the marker becomes a symbol of being in command. The typical scenario comes closer to the first one, though, where people want to be in charge during meetings but their commitment isn't necessarily strong enough to keep them involved and energized between sessions or when the collaboration encounters roadblocks or when their regular jobs demand their attention.

Being a committed leader of a value alliance is different from being a leader of a less collaborative entity, and the first difference involves the role of convener versus that of leader.

CONVENING VERSUS LEADING

What is the difference between a convener and a committed leader? Typically, conveners are individuals or groups with strong personal brands who initiate the collaboration. Committed leaders are those people who manage and move the collaboration forward. While conveners may also take on a leadership role, they often lack the time, capacity, or expertise necessary to be active and committed leaders. For this reason, they can designate others to preside over meetings and handle other collaborative managerial responsibilities. In some instances, leaders are selected by the group or naturally come to the forefront, but conveners who have the prerogative can select leaders with the unique talents required for building the proposed alliance.

In the largest organizations, conveners are often senior executives who catalyze the formation of a task force to deal with common pain affecting multiple units of their own organization. In other settings the same executive may act as a convener among external organizations that share the internal anxiety. While these executives may feel the pain, they may not have sufficient expertise to lead the problem-solving work—or they know individuals who are better known and more respected in this particular area than themselves. For example, a CEO of a midsized manufacturing company convened a collaboration in response to growing manufacturing safety concerns for factory line workers. This CEO was alarmed by a number of recent accidents in the company's factories, but his background in sales and marketing prevented him from grasping the technical details necessary to lead this collaboration effectively. For this reason, the CEO named a manufacturing vice president who was the company's top safety expert to take the lead. Not only did this individual possess the knowledge necessary to lead the group, his expertise and experience were greatly respected both in the company and throughout the industry. The convener was kept apprised of the group's progress and provided advice and resources to the leader, but he was not acting as the committed leader of the group itself.

In some instances, conveners stay out of the leadership role because they have higher-priority issues than the one the collaboration is focusing on. It's also possible that even though they recognize the value of collaboration to solve a problem, they aren't particularly interested in working on it. They are aware that they would be only partially committed as leader, and that this lack of total commitment could hurt the collaborative effort.

When it comes to the relationship between conveners and leaders, one of four scenarios usually plays out:

- The convener becomes the committed leader.
- The convener names a representative to be the committed leader.
- The convener appoints an independent leader.
- The group selects its own committed leader.

The Convener Becomes the Committed Leader

Some conveners perceive their group's goal to be of such high priority that they want to give it their personal attention. For example, when I convened the American Health Information Community (AHIC) as secretary of HHS, I viewed the initiative to develop an effective electronic medical record system as critical for reforming the U.S. health care system. Furthermore, I was concerned that the number and variety of vested interests would slow down or complicate the completion of these standards without my presence and involvement. The power of my convening brand was important, but so was my presence as a committed leader. There were obvious political risks if we didn't achieve our goals, and I burned lots of time in those meetings. But the industry knew I was serious and we got things done as a result.

The Convener Names a Representative to Be the Committed Leader

In this scenario, the convener defines the task, chooses the participants, and assembles them (perhaps working through assistants who execute these responsibilities). The convener of stature attends the first meeting and commissions someone (or perhaps more than one person) to act on the convener's behalf as committed leader. Periodically, the convener attends the meetings to receive reports from the group. Likewise, if problems require senior judgments, the commissioned committed leader seeks the convener's guidance.

This roughly describes the relationship between George Washington, James Madison, and Alexander Hamilton in assembling and managing the Constitutional Convention. While Washington's prestige and reputation helped him, among others, to convene the convention, the vision and elbow grease of Madison and Hamilton were what made it work. Washington actually sat in the room day after day to ensure that the delegations stayed on task.

The Convener Appoints an Independent Leader

Sometimes it is awkward for the convener to take the leadership role, because the constituencies the participants represent are suspicious of potential manipulation by the convener. In such circumstances it's apt to be more productive for the convener to step back and let someone else carry the load.

Recall the story of William, the university president described in Chapter Three, who convened an on-campus group to organize a new campuswide information technology initiative. It was politically important that the group not feel William was imposing a solution on them. For that reason, he appointed a committed leader he could trust while he oversaw the process. Periodically, William would receive updates and provide guidance, but the leader he appointed operated independently.

The Group Selects Its Own Committed Leader

In value alliances involving competing business interests or politically sensitive matters where public organizations are involved, it is wise to implement a transparent process for the group to select its leader. In many cases, the group selects two or even three committed leaders from various sides of an issue. Be aware that when a value alliance is led by two or three competitors, various dynamics can come into play. For instance, small competitors may resolve not to allow a dominant player in the market to be the leader or resent it when it happens, or ideological foes may lobby to have a trusted third party lead.

THE RANGE OF RESPONSIBILITIES

In some ways, committed leadership is even more important in value alliances than in established hierarchical organizations. An alliance is held together with loose threads. As a new entity, it lacks a history, culture, and decision-making structure to facilitate implementation. More important, a new network is generally a collaboration among equals. Lacking a clear pecking order, networks need leaders to step forward and facilitate the decision-making process, and they require leaders who display a flexibility that may not be needed in more traditional corporate structures. It's one thing to direct subordinates to create solutions and implement them; it's another thing to motivate—in the absence of authority—a diverse group of experts, senior executives, government officials, and consumer advocates to carry out the same tasks.

For this reason, committed leaders can't just be order-givers; nor can they just be facilitators, communicators, strategists, or motivators. They must possess a greater range than the average leader to ensure execution. For instance, one or more collaborative partners may threaten to leave the table. Perhaps they become impatient with the lack of progress, or they feel estranged because their concerns aren't being adequately addressed or for other reasons. No formal structure or obligation mandates their continued participation. While they certainly feel the common pain and want to eliminate or minimize it, they may decide that they're better able to do so outside the collaboration, or that their frustration with the collaborative group is worse than the pain they're feeling.

In these instances, committed leaders might draw on their authority to insist their fellow collaborators stay the course and to bring potential defectors back to the fold. They remind everyone how the pain will grow and hurt these individuals' organizations unless the collaboration comes up with a viable solution. They may argue passionately and forcibly from a position of commitment, reminding other participants of why they came together in the first place.

At other times, committed leaders must coax, flatter, and nudge wavering participants in the right direction. Instead of proclaiming or intimidating, they must speak softly and persuasively for the good of the group. One senior executive from a large corporation was part of a coalition put together to research cutting-edge technologies in their industry. This executive had a natural command-and-control style as a leader in his corporation. But when the coalition stalled because of disagreements among participants about the best technological alternatives to pursue, a few key participants threatened to withdraw. This executive used a quiet, personal approach to persuade them to give the coalition a few additional months to see if they could come up with a viable position. He never tried to intimidate the people who were on the cusp of resigning, instead using quiet, persistent logic that encouraged them to stay on board and give the collaboration more of a chance. He communicated his commitment to the group by making an extra effort—he took people on the fence out to dinner or for drinks and spoke sincerely and convincingly about why they should stay. His effort was sufficient to nudge people back on board, at least for a few critical months.

This leader succeeded not only by making an extra effort but by demonstrating his commitment. In every value alliance we've been associated with or observed, the best leaders have demonstrated an unusual degree of involvement and passion for the collaborative effort. By modeling behavior that demonstrates the importance of the work the group is doing, leaders communicate how invested they are in the value alliance's goals. Committed leaders show up for meetings and treat them seriously. They make a visible effort to secure resources, to suggest solutions, to inspire others. In this way, they not only get things done on behalf of the collaboration but motivate others to work hard for its objectives.

Value alliances require committed leaders who fulfill many of these ten roles:

- *Organizer*. Without benefit of a hierarchical structure or tested processes and procedures, leaders must prepare concise agendas, send meeting reminders, prepare documents, and arrange the meeting room. While they may have subordinates who execute these functions, the leaders themselves are responsible for making sure the tasks are completed properly and on time.
- *Diplomat*. Because of the diversity of those in a collaboration, diplomacy is often required to ease tensions between competitors and other unhappy associates. For instance, in a given collaboration, a consumer activist and a business executive were both participants, though the activist has been a vocal opponent of the executive's company for years. In other instances, the tensions are more subtle—say, an Ivy League–educated investment banker has difficulty relating to a community organizer who dropped out of high school. Committed leaders take it upon themselves to smooth the obvious and subtle tensions. Many times, it's as simple as facilitating informal discussions between the two parties—once they get to know each other on a personal level, the tension dissipates. In other instances, however, long-standing animosity between two individuals means that the committed leader must make an ongoing effort to keep the relationship productive.
- *Technician*. In most instances, expertise of some kind (and often, many kinds) is critical for solving a problem. While committed leaders may not be technical experts themselves, they must take responsibility for bringing that expertise to bear on the problem, wherever it exists. This means they must possess some knowledge of the technical issues, even if they lack the skill to implement a solution. This knowledge will

enable them to find the experts—either within the collaborative group or outside it—and direct them to work on the issue at hand.

• *Teacher*. At the very least, committed leaders need to educate representatives about the problem and the solutions that have been tried in the past. Again, they may not be leading authorities on a subject, but it's their job to present an overview that everyone can understand and relate to. These leaders must make sure that everyone is aware of the severity of the problem and why it needs to be addressed collectively—this serves to create commitment among the participants.

• *Counselor*. The participants may have problems that require advice. In one instance, a participant was concerned about all the time his work with the collaboration was taking and that he was neglecting his responsibilities at his day job. He wasn't sure what to tell his employer, who while in favor of participation had also expressed reservations about the time commitment. The committed leader knew the CEO at the participant's company and offered to talk to him about the issue. While committed leaders may be able to deal with participants' issues directly, as in this instance, many times they can help by simply being good listeners and delivering feedback. In this way, they can keep people focused on the issues the collaboration was convened to address.

• *Matchmaker*. Within a collaboration, opportunities exist for introducing disparate groups to one another and having them work synergistically on an aspect of a problem. For instance, a Fortune 100 corporation executive and the founder of a small, highly successful start-up were in the same collaborative group, and the committed leader recognized that the start-up founder's innovative brilliance could be best used to solve the problem facing the group if he had superior technological resources—resources the Fortune 100 company had in abundance. Committed leaders, therefore, should be aware of the capabilities and resources of every participant and then be able to match them in order to maximize their contributions.

• *Salesperson*. Not all leaders are natural-born salespeople, but value alliances require committed leaders to convince a number of people to do a number of things. So if selling is not a natural skill, committed leaders need to make an effort to become proficient at it, at least in certain areas. First and foremost, committed leaders need to convince and remind participants of the value of their mission. Though every participant is participating because of self-interest—it is in their (and often, their organization's) best interest to solve the problem that is causing the common pain—sometimes they need reminding of this fact. Leaders must make convincing arguments that counteract the frustration that arises from delays and or setbacks. In addition, committed leaders may need to sell participants on investing more time, energy, and resources in the collaborative effort. And third, they may need to sell participants on a particular course of action—on agreeing on a recommendation or strategy.

• *Referee*. Though they may be diverse in background, expertise, and perspective, representatives of substance are often used to being obeyed. Consequently, when they come together in a diverse collaborative group, conflicts arise. Committed leaders shouldn't attempt to stifle debate or resolve every conflict immediately—productive ideas often emerge from the friction between clashing points of view. Leaders should, however, referee debates between members so the debates are productive rather than destructive. This means calling fouls (when one member attacks personally rather than professionally), signaling time-outs (when tension is high and everyone needs a break), and making sure the game is played by the rules (no backroom deals).

• *Judge*. What's the best recommendation? Who should serve as point person for the group's main project? What method is best for obtaining the needed information? While a collaboration requires a lot of different voices to be heard, at some point, decisions must be made. Committed leaders have to make a number of judgment calls or the collaboration can suffer from analysis paralysis and other stalemates. Committed leaders judge in order to keep the collaboration moving forward. They hear opposing arguments and then determine which makes the most sense. While leaders should follow a participatory decision-making process, instances occur where they must judge the best idea or option or risk wasting time and increasing frustration.

- *Disciplinarian.* Effective value alliances don't have obstructionists and saboteurs. That's because committed leaders identify participants who are gumming up the works and do something about them. Even though leaders in collaborative settings lack the level of control and power they might have in an established organization, they still possess sufficient authority to discipline participants who are impeding the group's progress. In some instances, discipline may be nothing more than talking privately to the offender about the disruptive behaviors. There are situations, though, when a participant is sabotaging the group's efforts. It may be inadvertent sabotage (by people who are so argumentative or contrarian that they make it impossible to reach a decision) or it may be deliberate (by people who have grown disenchanted with the collaboration and hope it doesn't survive long enough to take action), but committed leaders must deal with these character traits that make it difficult for the collaboration to achieve its goal. While cynics and critics can add constructive value, saboteurs' efforts to undermine the effort require discipline or removal.

COMMITTED LEADERS WE HAVE KNOWN

Value alliances always seem to have at least one leader who demonstrates the ten traits we list here. Commencing in 1997 Bruce Johnson (in his role as a state tax commissioner) was involved in the group that eventually became the Streamlined Sales Tax Project. He was an organizer, a technician, a matchmaker, and more. This was an extraordinarily complex collaboration involving many different disciplines and states, and as a committed leader, he helped people persevere through the complexities. During meetings and in individual discussions with participants, he kept pointing out the larger picture—the benefits of creating a more equitable tax structure—and his efforts kept participants at the table who might otherwise have left during the slow-moving and at times frustrating process.

Vice Admiral Conrad C. Lautenbacher, the convener of GEOSS, demonstrated many of the committed leader traits, especially that of referee. When you have a collaboration that consists of leaders from countries that have historical and current tensions, you have to be skilled at managing the conflicts that arise during discussions and keep the focus on the collaborative goal rather than on personal and political animosity. As a top military officer as well as a true expert on oceans and atmosphere issues, he could use the respect his career conferred to moderate the tensions that sometimes threatened to sidetrack discussions.

Roger Tew, an attorney and tax expert, demonstrated how these ten traits can drive a collaboration to solve huge problems. Prior to the formal formation of the International Fuel Tax Agreement Association (IFTA) in 1991, the truck transport industry was laboring under a highly inefficient system that created many problems and much pain both for trucking companies and for the various states. Each state had its own fuel tax system, and every truck had to have individual tax permits and license plates for every state in which it operated—and when operating in more than one jurisdiction, trucking companies had to report and pay taxes separately in each of them. As a result, the industry was saddled with an expensive administrative system. There were many other issues, but the states and the trucking industry were hurting and needed to ease their pain.[1]

Roger Tew was the driving force behind the creation of IFTA—like Vice Admiral Lautenbacher, he was both convener of stature and committed leader. An organizer, salesperson, teacher, and technician, Roger wore many hats as a committed leader. One of the challenges was simply dealing with the incredibly confusing tax laws, and his ability to understand and explain these laws to IFTA members was invaluable. But perhaps most important, he had to get all the right people to participate in IFTA or they would never be able to come up with and implement a solution. That solution—which involved allowing carriers to file a single tax return in their official home state—required formation of an operational group that possessed sufficient clout as well as technical expertise. Roger, as head of IFTA, was able to recruit the technicians as representatives to deal with the tax issues, but he also had to use this influence and powers of persuasion to recruit diverse individuals with the authority to implement the proposed solution. He was able to bring in commissioner-level and operations-level representatives to join the board and secured a strong mix of people from state transportation and revenue departments. Perhaps most important, Roger used his influence and persuasiveness to convince all participants from various states to trust each other's auditing procedures (an essential step in implementing the tax agreement).

Because of Roger's efforts, all forty-eight contiguous states joined the collaboration and implemented the agreement, which remains in place to this day. It's fair to say that without Roger's leadership, this agreement would not have been implemented and the pain would have continued for years.

Like Roger Tew, Conrad Lautenbacher, and Bruce Johnson, committed leaders often need to wear a number of hats, use their influence to keep the collaboration together (at least until a problem is solved), and work very, very hard. These leaders often have other jobs, and so it's asking a lot for them to work overtime heading a coalition for which they may not be getting paid. It may require the persistence and even the bullheadedness of one or more leaders to pull the collaboration through to the point where it can put its recommendations to work.

THE CONSENSUS QUESTION

A value alliance is a powerful instrument for the same reason it is a fragile one—voluntary participation. It is the invisible hand of the idea marketplace that brings order to this collaborative but voluntary democracy. If participants ever feel their best interest is served by leaving, they can and will leave. If at any point the consensus tips too far in one direction, a critical mass of participants will withdraw, and the value alliance will quickly die. Yet if committed leaders can consistently achieve consensus, they will move the alliance forward.

Finding consensus is an art form that alliance leaders must master. There are times when a collaborative leader will be challenged by participants threatening to leave if they don't get their way. Such a leader may stretch the patience of participants who favor one side of an issue in order to keep other participants involved. It is a tricky balancing act but one that is preferable to majority voting.

Despite the admiration for voting ingrained in U.S. culture, it turns out that making decisions on the basis of majority rule is often divisive in a collaborative setting, as it can polarize rather than unify—and polarization is antithetical to the operational and structural nature of a collaborative entity. In addition, the debate leading up to a vote can become highly antagonistic and may provoke the losing group to walk out of the collaboration or to lose interest and engagement. For this reason, we have developed a set of simple rules for consensus building.

Committed leaders are responsible for facilitating recommendations and decisions that solve the problem the group is dealing with. Part of the challenge for these leaders is that they lack the position power to select the idea they believe in and push it through. They can't simply declare, "We're going to recommend Option A because it's the one I think will work best." In a collaborative democracy, consensus rules, and committed leaders need to be masters of consensus-based decision making. Because consensus invites discussion, listening is amplified as the alliance attempts to find a solution rather than advocate a position. Every voice, therefore, becomes important. Rather than count votes the leader will typically say, "I sense that we have consensus on this issue. Does anyone feel differently or have more to say?" The impact on the group dynamics can be dramatic.

Therefore, committed leaders may find the following consensus-building rules useful:

Nothing is final until the collaborative process is complete. This allows participants to feel more comfortable with the process moving forward even though they object to a particular choice or direction. Participants will have the ability to examine the totality of the proposed solution before deciding if it is acceptable or not. At the conclusion of the collaborative process, the committed leader will attempt to gain as much consensus as possible on the value alliance decision document.

Consensus doesn't require unanimous agreement, but it does require a willingness to compromise, concede, or step aside. Essentially, this allows value alliances to move forward even when one or more of the representatives disagree with a plan or decision. People may voice their dissenting opinions but they refrain from becoming impediments to progress.

Leaders are responsible for crafting and declaring a consensus and asking if there are objections. As you might imagine, crafting a consensus involves relying on some or all of the ten committed leader functions—organizer, diplomat, salesperson, referee, and so on. While in a majority democracy, the leader wants everyone to adhere to a given plan or point of view once it's been voted in regardless of what they think about it; in a collaborative democracy, the leader makes an effort to achieve the widest possible acceptance. To do so, committed leaders must know the participants' views, priorities, and strength of conviction. It may be that a dissenter holds to that point of view with only moderate force and has other priorities that a leader may accommodate; this knowledge helps the leader determine the best possible strategy for consensus-building. Similarly, a leader who asks for objections and receives one may take that objection into consideration and possibly reformulate the consensus decision or recommendation with that objection in mind.

Committed leaders have the option of declaring a "near consensus" when expressed objections make a full consensus impossible. A near consensus means that objections are noted but that the objecting parties agree to move forward with the plan or decision that most people agree upon without declaring impasse or dropping out of the collaborative group. The parameters of declaring a near consensus should be spelled out in the formal charter (a written document stating the goals and working parameters of a collaboration, as discussed in Chapter Seven), specifying that a super-majority is required (almost everyone agrees on the decision).

Committed leaders can declare an impasse when consensus or near consensus isn't achieved. In other words, they can set the issue aside but have the option of revisiting it at a later date. It's possible that new developments will cause those who raised objections to change their views; it's also possible that committed leaders can work behind the scenes to communicate with objectors or find ways to reshape a recommendation so that it's acceptable to all. When everyone knows and agrees that committed leaders can declare an impasse and that they have the option of bringing the matter up again later, they are essentially agreeing to reconsider their opinions at some point in the future. This creates a more open-minded approach to decision making than usually prevails in more adversarial groups.

We understand that relying on this consensus decision-making model may seem cumbersome, especially to heads of organizations accustomed to a more authoritative approach. What we would ask is that you think about the collaborative environment as different from the traditional organizational one and recognize that the role of leader changes somewhat in this environment as they try to stimulate discussion and ensure that all have been heard rather than making decisions. In a more diverse, participatory, voluntary culture, consensus becomes a higher priority—a priority committed leaders recognize and integrate into the way they run their groups.

SIX

A Clearly Defined Purpose

Creating a statement of purpose, communicating it, and obtaining buy-in from participants can be challenging, but they're absolutely essential tasks for value alliance aspirants. Without a clear, well-defined purpose, collaborations fail or drift into unproductive and endless discussions. More specifically, the collaborations experience *purpose creep*—an inexorable broadening of scope that eventually makes it impossible to relieve the common pain that drew the group together in the first place, or that creates lethally low morale as the collaboration struggles with overly ambitious and varied goals. Without a clearly articulated and written purpose (which will then be incorporated in the formal charter), each representative of substance may define the purpose differently. These varying definitions stem more from human nature than any deliberate malice or selfishness: everyone involved wants a collaboration to meet the needs of their primary affiliation—their corporate, government, or nonprofit employer. Unless the real purpose is articulated, memorialized, and ratified by the participants, they will all shape it with bias toward their own parochial interests.

Here's an example of what happens when purpose isn't clearly defined from the outset. Twenty business competitors come together to reduce the common pain of what they feel are increasingly stringent government regulations regarding product quality; meanwhile, the government is considering legislation that imposes extremely tough regulations because one company's lax quality control resulted in a number of product failures. The offending company has declared bankruptcy and is not a part of this collaboration. Because the competitors are in a rush to provide an alternative to the pending legislation, they dispense with a discussion of purpose (as well as the creation of a charter) at their first meeting, agreeing verbally that their goal is to defeat this legislation by offering a more viable alternative under the current law.

Despite great enthusiasm and participation at this first meeting, problems quickly emerge. Representatives from the larger companies and the smaller companies clash over alternative proposals; the larger companies favor provisions that require a significant investment in improved quality control while smaller companies complain they can't afford such a large expenditure and would rather have government oversight and inspection take care of it for them. In addition, representatives of companies with the best quality control processes in place favor punitive governmental measures for organizations without high-level quality mechanisms; the companies that lack state-of-the-art processes believe this position reflects bias. The collaboration dissolves in discord before diminishing the common pain.

Perhaps the participants would not have achieved their objective even if they had defined and ratified it at the beginning—the purpose gaps between participants might have been too great to overcome even then—their chances of success would have been much better if they had found common purpose. People are more motivated to compromise in the initial stages, when enthusiasm is high and pain is intense. Later in the collaboration, if they feel their fellow collaborators have misled them about purpose, they are much less willing to find common ground.

SUCCESSFUL PURPOSE STATEMENTS

The purpose statements of successful value alliances—and for all the value alliances featured in this book—are clear, specific, goal-focused, and relatively short. While some purpose statements may carry a whiff of legalese (or in a few cases, more than a whiff) because they are part of a legal document or because lawyers had a hand in writing them, they generally provide an easy-to-understand and accurate summary of what the collaboration is trying to achieve.

Here is a sampling of these statements (either taken from the formal charter or our interpretation of the purpose communicated to the collaboration):

- IFTA: To enable more uniformity and cooperation with regard to the reporting and payment of motor carrier fuel use taxes. Implementation of the International Fuel Tax Agreement.[1]
- Magnetic Ink Character Recognition: Develop a font and computerized system that would allow for check automation, [promote] standardization of checks, and reduce check fraud.[2]
- GEOSS: Achieve sustained operation, continuity, and interoperability of existing and new systems that provide essential environmental observations and information, including the GEOSS Common Infrastructure that facilitates access to, and use of, these observations and information.[3]
- GHX: Automate the supply chain process and engage in management of relevant data (contract terms, catalogs, and item masters).[4]
- AHIC: Make recommendations to the Secretary of the U.S. Department of Health and Human Services on how to accelerate the development and adoption of health information technology.[5]

With hindsight, these purpose statements seem obvious. In the heat of the moment, though, it's a challenge to find the language that will communicate and motivate clearly.

A LIFE-SAVING PURPOSE

A compelling and clear purpose focuses the minds of collaborators like little else and helps them overcome whatever differences lie between them. Here is a vivid example:

I was secretary of HHS in 2005 when President George W. Bush convened a collaboration that had one of the most dynamic purposes of any group I've been associated with: To restore and improve vaccine capacity in the event of a pandemic. This combination of social benefits—an effort to save what might well amount to millions of lives—and economic incentives helped our collaboration achieve great success and decrease the likelihood of significant common pain.

As background, historical records show an average of three pandemics per century—disrupting communities, families, businesses, and economies. By 2005 the world had become concerned about the emergence of H5N1 Avian Flu, which appeared to be developing in Japan, Vietnam, Thailand, Hong Kong, and the Philippines. When influenza becomes transmissible from person to person, it is a risk everywhere because it can spread quickly and efficiently throughout the world. Meanwhile, U.S. scientists had been concerned about our national lack of preparedness for years. The H5N1 virus outbreak and its attendant national risk created obvious common pain that required a response. Despite its wealth of scientific knowledge and unparalleled ability to plan for a rapidly spreading disease, the reality was that the country was actually no better prepared in 2005 than it had been in 1918.

President Bush was acutely aware of these and other facts, which is why he signed an Executive Order (on November 1, 2005) at an event at the National Institutes of Health. The Executive Order detailed the problems related to lack of preparedness for a pandemic and appointed me to lead the effort to do something about it.[6] Understandably, when a president convenes, a collaboration quickly gains momentum, and that is precisely what happened.

In subsequent months I worked with the White House, HHS, and other Cabinet colleagues to formulate a strategic response that would address the major and numerous weaknesses in our defense against influenza. Work commenced with the Homeland Security Council, which was the lead on developing a national preparedness plan. We developed a doctrine of war against a pandemic that recognized sustained person-to-person transmission of flu anywhere as a threat everywhere. Our aspiration was for this generation to be the first in world history to prepare for and successfully mitigate a pandemic. We anticipated that in the global economy, disease containment in countries of origin would ultimately fail, and that left us with the assumption that we would have no more than six weeks before an outbreak that started in Asia would reach the United States.

As part of our effort, we needed localities, businesses, and families to be better prepared. I traveled to thirty-eight states, while other HHS leaders went to the remaining states and territories to raise awareness and to ask state and local governments together with their citizens to think through their outbreak response plans. We met with the press, with bloggers, and with public and private entities across the country.

John Barry's *The Great Influenza: The Story of the Deadliest Pandemic in History* played a major role in the effort. I read and marked the sections I thought most critical, then deployed a member of our staff to underline and tab those sections for participants.[7] Barry's eloquent words reminded everyone of our mission and its importance. The highlighted passages became a great tool in working with members of Congress, the Cabinet, and even some governors, allowing these busy officials to read and absorb key sections quickly.

Our purpose drove us to improve vaccine production. In 2005 the capacity to produce vaccine in the United States was limited. For logical economic reasons, manufacturing capacity had moved offshore. But reliance in an emergency on production from companies in Europe was neither prudent nor efficient, and we simply did not have adequate U.S.-based production capacity. Additionally, at that time influenza vaccine relied upon eggs for production. Every dose came from a single chicken egg, which meant that production capacity was limited by the supply of eggs. While we needed to expand egg-based production capacity by retrofitting existing plants, we also needed to develop new technologies to establish production methods that would shorten the time to manufacture vaccines, increase scalability, and eliminate reliance on one-egg-one-dose production. This longer-term solution was referred to as cell-based technology.

This kind of problem required a special kind of expertise. I convened a group of experts within HHS and asked them to tackle those two very specific problems—expanding present egg-based capacity and developing cell-based technologies. Charlie Johnson (assistant secretary for resources and technology) and his deputy Tom Reilly, along with Robin Roberts (director of the Biomedical Advanced Research Development Authority) and Bill Raub (my science adviser) led this part of the effort. This team built alliances throughout HHS and the federal government, met at least weekly, created accountability, and focused on the task with laser-like clarity, never deviating from their purpose. When lives are at stake—and everyone recognizes this as the reason for the group's existence—focus comes naturally.

The clearly defined purpose of this effort was influenced by many factors. At its core was the preservation of lives and the power of the purse. Federal money reduced the risk for private sector investment and created an incentive where the market had lacked sufficient pull. In 2006 we awarded more than $1 billion in contracts to six companies to help accomplish our objectives. Each participating company had a government contract supervisor who stayed very connected and reported at least weekly on its progress. Charlie and his team constructed an interesting visual. A literal horse race, posted on the wall in his budget office, showed the progress of each company, represented by a horse, to keep them focused on the objective.

I'm happy to report that we accomplished this part of the mission. U.S. vaccine production capacity improved significantly, and on November 20, 2012, Novartis received FDA approval for the first cell-culture vaccine, in what some described as the most significant advancement in vaccine manufacturing in forty years.[8] While faster and higher-volume production is important, there is still much to be done with regard to shortening the time to develop a viable vaccine and improving the effectiveness of vaccines—especially for those over sixty-five years of age. Without such scientific improvements related to effectiveness, pandemic influenza could still cause catastrophic problems. Thankfully, the capacity and production speed to manufacture is significantly improved.

THREE TIME PERIODS

While it's sometimes relatively easy to establish and secure agreement on a purpose—especially when a group is temporary and designed to disband upon solving a specific problem—it's safer to expect to devote time to the effort. The process of forging a purpose can begin before the collaboration even exists, then continue when it first convenes and in subsequent meetings. Attention to these three time frames will help create a well-defined purpose.

Before the Collaboration

Conveners can use a declaration of purpose as a trial balloon to see who it attracts to the coalition that is forming. More proactively, they can shape the purpose to attract the right people to the table. In some instances, we've convened collaborations in which we've framed the purpose carefully while recruiting representatives of substance to address the issues of most concern to them. If, for instance, you want to form a collaboration designed to address a growing environmental problem, you may deem it vital to bring all the companies responsible for contributing to the problem into the collaboration. If your declared purpose is to end the environmental devastation immediately regardless of cost or consequences, you probably won't draw in a company that is contributing to environmental problems. But if the purpose is cleaning up the environment in a socially responsible way while removing obstacles to profit and growth, then that company is likely to see it as an inducement to join.

The wording of the preliminary declaration of purpose can actually kill a collaboration before it's begun. On more than one occasion, I've had people tell me: "If you're going to define the purpose this way, then it's not in our interest to join. We prefer the status quo." Be aware, too, that people may not be this upfront in their refusal; they may offer a credible excuse (say, too many other commitments) when in fact their problem is the way you've framed the purpose.

89

Conveners can and should use the power to declare a purpose to facilitate collaborative sign-ups. Doing so isn't presumptuous; it is the prerogative of the convening role. While the declared purpose may evolve a bit once the collaboration begins and people negotiate the wording, the right purpose declared compellingly at an early stage can galvanize support, energy, and commitment.

When I was governor of Utah, I wanted to build a major highway in the middle of the state, a project that would cost a significant amount of money. I recognized that I would face opposition, especially among people and legislators who lived in parts of the state that wouldn't be served by the new highway. I was also aware that if the highway were constructed the traditional way, it would take almost ten years to complete and would almost certainly turn into a mess resembling Boston's "Big Dig" project.

For this project to gain legislative support, we needed to create a collaboration. No contractor in the state had the capacity to construct this highway with the speed and economy necessary to win approval. For this reason, we created a competition, challenging diverse organizations in the state to form collaborative entities to bid for the project. Up front, I made the purpose of the collaboration clear: to design and build the highway so as to accelerate completion and reduce costs. This design-build purpose motivated four different collaborative groups to form, and each of the four groups consisted of architects, contractors, public relations agencies, and other specialized functions. We also offered a $1 million incentive if these groups could demonstrate the capacity to handle the design-build approach. Ultimately, one collaboration rose above the rest; we chose it for the project, and it completed the job in four and a half years and millions of dollars under budget.

While this collaboration was motivated by many factors (including the millions in incentives we paid for speed and savings), the well-defined statement of purpose was a magnet that drew diverse entities into a collaboration and then guided their efforts every step of the way.

At the Initial Meeting

Traditionally, the convener or committed leader introduces the purpose during the first meeting of collaborative partners, or it arises from discussion during the meeting. Ideally, a clear, focused purpose is agreed upon and put in writing in the group's charter.

Many times, however, the act of stating the official purpose creates not just discussion but debate. Value alliances are strong enough to accommodate vigorous disagreements, but committed leaders need to keep these debates focused on principles, goals, and methods rather than allowing them to become personal. When people start prefacing their arguments by accusing their fellow representatives of being closed-minded or selfish, the seeds of the collaboration's destruction are sown.

For instance, when the governors of western states convened a collaboration to create a shared doctrine of environmental management, it took a while to come up with a statement of purpose. Some participants leaned more toward policies that favored revenue generated by natural resources over conservation while others sought to protect the environment no matter what the cost. Therefore, when we met, we needed a purpose that kept everyone at the table and motivated to find a solution to the environment-related challenges our states were facing. Ultimately, we came together on the following statement of purpose:

Today there is no symbol for the middle, for the majority of citizens who believe that the environment and its natural resources can be protected while at the same time providing recreational and employment opportunities for citizens. Doctrine provides a collection of tools, that, if employed, will result in improved and expedited environmental decision-making and implementation.[9]

This statement of purpose was followed by a set of principles that provided a set of beliefs behind this purpose and a "hope" statement that reinforced how the purpose was to be followed and the goals of adhering to this purpose. Through this approach, we were able to address the concerns of multiple interests and keep all the requisite players involved and deeply committed from the start.

The biggest mistake committed leaders can make regarding purpose in this initial session is to decide that no purpose statement is necessary. It may be that the argument about purpose is threatening to spiral out of control, and so the leader tables the discussion to avoid greater conflict; or it may be that the purpose seems obvious and that no formal discussion or written statement about it is necessary. Whatever the justification, the lack of a purpose statement articulated in the charter is often the fatal flaw in collaborations—or at least the factor that prevents them from becoming value alliances.

I've alluded to the frustration I felt as secretary of HHS after Hurricane Katrina when I convened and led the Louisiana Health Care Collaborative, a group designed to reform the health care system in Louisiana. It failed, in part because we lacked a sufficient number of representatives of substance. But it also failed because we were never able to articulate and agree upon a singular purpose. Vested interests in the established Charity Hospital System preferred making small changes but maintaining the status quo. Some of us, however, wanted to make more sweeping changes that eliminated the low-quality health care services that the status quo ensured. We moved forward without consensus on whether we were going to make small changes or sweeping ones. As a result, we did neither and the collaboration fell apart.

Of course, it is sometimes impossible to establish and formalize a purpose during an initial meeting. If that's the case, don't ignore the issue—attempt to create a purpose over the next few meetings.

By Negotiation

As representatives get to know each other and as the committed leader gets to know the representatives, it often becomes easier to negotiate a purpose than it was during the initial session when people were feeling each other out and wary of individuals they either didn't know or regarded as competitors. In addition, when a collaboration is first convened, people tend to gravitate toward generalities. Out of politeness or perhaps out of distrust, people aren't willing to commit themselves to a specific purpose statement.

It's up to the committed leader to move participants toward a purpose statement through negotiation during the first two or three meetings. In doing so, the leader needs to work for a statement that is focused, clear, and pain-reducing—and set in terms that won't drive away key participants. If a purpose emerges that doesn't seem worth certain participants' time and energy, they'll depart—and retaining them can be worthwhile, as our own national history shows. Initially, the issue of slavery was on the table at the Constitutional Convention, but it became clear to the leaders of the convention that resolving slavery was impossible—that if this were part of the purpose, it would drive away too many representatives of substance. After a series of negotiations, slavery was not addressed. And despite the troubles that followed, resulting in war three-quarters of a century later, few would argue that the work of the convention was not worthwhile. It did prove able to deal with the common pain that had drawn the participants together.

Collaboration requires a strong leader to work toward a consensus purpose, rather than allowing the purpose to be hijacked—imposed on the group by an influential, aggressive participant using force of personality and clout. A hijacked purpose can be worse than a vague one. For instance, a high school and the collaborative group that formed to help fund work on the track facility and to install lights (a simple "lights and lanes" funding project) made progress by recruiting a range of representatives of substance, including local business leaders and some nationally known track athletes. One prominent business leader, however, had a vision that went beyond our original concept for the collaboration. Rather than just upgrade the facilities, he saw the possibility of creating a state-of-the-art track facility, holding international track events there, and earning significant amounts of money from this facility by turning his hometown into a major track-and-field center.

As ambitious and as visionary as this business leader's plan was, it essentially destroyed the collaboration's ability to hold together. The collaboration began without a formal charter or clear articulation of purpose—we just assumed that everyone understood what our relatively modest goal was. Over time, however, as new members joined the group, the initial purpose faded into the background. As a result, this business leader was able to expand the purpose of the group far beyond its original aim. This created confusion and conflict, and in its wake, many participants lost their enthusiasm and commitment, causing the collaboration to disband.

HOW TO COLLABORATE PURPOSEFULLY: A STEP-BY-STEP GUIDE

There is much talk these days of living a purposeful life, and while just about everyone agrees with the sentiment, achieving the result can be a challenge. How do you discover your purpose? How do you use this discovery to guide your actions? How do you avoid swerving from the path your purpose lays out for you?

The same questions that can be asked about individual purpose can be asked from a collaborative perspective. To use purpose so that a collaboration becomes a value alliance, you need a guide. Here are seven steps that will you develop a purpose in a collaborative setting:

1. Begin with a problem-solving, pain-mitigating mindset.
2. Frame problems and pain judiciously.
3. Match purpose to representatives' capabilities.
4. Create the purpose through discussion and consensus (rather than brainstorming and politicking).
5. Be flexible in the type of purpose statement you create.
6. Put the purpose in writing and in participants' consciousness.
7. Have a process in place to revise or reformulate the purpose.

Step One

Begin with a problem-solving, pain-mitigating mindset.

The convener, committed leader, and representatives need to look at the pain they're experiencing to discover their purpose. The clues to purpose are contained in the issue that brings diverse people together. For instance, the Great Lakes Regional Collaboration formed because participants were suffering from the increasing pollution of their waterways. The collaboration's purpose, therefore, was to "enhance the U.S. efforts to restore and protect the Great Lakes ecosystem."[10] A discussion of the cause of pain and what will alleviate it is the best way to find purpose.

Step Two

Frame problems and pain judiciously.

By *judiciously*, we mean making sure that the purpose directly aligns with the problem or that it is focused realistically on what can be accomplished to diminish the pain. As noted, collaborations' reach may exceed their grasp—they find it tempting to take on more than they have the capacity to achieve. It's also possible that they become sidetracked on a sexy issue that is related to the problem but doesn't provide an effective solution.

For instance, suppose a collaboration of law firms, police, and citizen groups work together to address the problem of wrongful convictions. In poor inner-city communities and rural areas, especially, the rate for wrongful convictions is high, resulting not only in pain and suffering for the wrongfully convicted individuals and their families but negative publicity for police and the legal system, as well as significant financial costs (of prosecutions, appeals, retrials, and so on). During the initial meeting, however, one of the law firm's managing partners volunteers to have his in-house software design team create a website that will provide all types of resources for wrongfully convicted individuals. All the participants are excited about this possibility, and each takes on a role to help get the website up and running and communicate its existence through media publicity and advertising. The group's purpose, therefore, centers on website dissemination of useful information for the wrongfully convicted. This is a good thing to do, yet it will not alleviate much of the pain the group set out to address, which is rooted in poor police investigation procedures, inadequate legal resources for the poor, and so on. Yet the website is something tangible that everyone can rally around, and so the purpose is misaligned.

In our work with the Environmental Protection Agency, we found that collaborations are much better able to overcome bounded problems than fuzzy issues. In other words, when the purpose imposes boundaries around how a problem will be tackled, it's more likely that the group will achieve its objective than when the purpose is generalized.

Step Three

Match purpose to representatives' capabilities.

Even representatives of real substance may lack the knowledge, skills, money, or other resources to deliver optimum results for a collaboration. Yet in that enthusiastic rush of the initial meeting, participants may set the bar too high. When we convened the group that became Western Governors University, we could have set the bar higher than we did. But instead of aiming to revolutionize the U.S. higher educational system or creating a target of 10 million online college students in five years, we settled on the more modest purpose of disrupting the educational status quo through an online university alternative. Our collaboration was working under financial limitations and personnel constraints—we had prestigious representatives from various sectors, but the group was small—so we set a purpose that was appropriate to our capabilities.

This doesn't mean that you can't modify or create a new purpose as circumstances dictate, after the first one has been achieved or after more representatives with greater resources join. Initially, however, leaders need to assess their group's collective capabilities and match them to a purpose.

Step Four

Create the purpose through discussion and consensus (rather than brainstorming and politicking).

If discussions of purpose devolve into partisanship and wide-ranging talks about every subject under the sun, it will be difficult to find and state a value alliance–catalyzing purpose. The former approach is overly divisive and the latter tends to produce a laundry list of purposes.

We are advocates of consensus and near-consensus decision making because they help avoid the divisiveness of majority voting as well as the stalemates that can plague diverse collaborative groups. In the Western Governors University collaboration, we had a wide variety of interests, but consensus helped us reach a statement of common purpose relatively quickly.

As you might imagine, the self-interest that motivated participants to join WGU varied quite a bit. The tech companies wanted to increase their supply of skillful young programmers and related professionals. The governors wanted to find a lower-cost online alternative to traditional higher education. But even though their motivations were different, they found common purpose. The overarching goal of shaking up the status quo with a new approach to online education resonated with all participants. When you're in a similar situation, don't worry if your participants all have their own particular reasons for being in the collaboration. If you find a strong purpose that is focused and relates to their particular problems, you can achieve consensus.

Step Five

Be flexible in the type of purpose statement you create.

This may seem like an obvious point, but Rich and I have seen groups try to boil their purpose down to one sentence when the complexity of their endeavor required a longer statement; we've also seen long-winded purpose paragraphs that could have been boiled down to one sentence. Don't be hamstrung by rules about length or style.

Be aware, too, that you may be involved in a collaboration that requires an initial purpose statement that will be reformulated when the collaboration redefines itself; or that your limited-time, single-purpose collaboration requires a simple statement while your more wide-ranging, ongoing collaboration requires a purpose statement supplemented by principles (as with the doctrine of environmental management described earlier in the chapter).

Your collaboration may be dealing with complex issues, but putting forth a convoluted, meandering statement of purpose isn't beneficial. There's no point in covering all the issues at the expense of comprehensibility. In these instances, it may be wise to provide a simple statement of purpose and supplement it with explanatory statements.

The Streamlined Sales Tax Governing Board was created to deal with the common pain of Internet retailers' gaining an advantage over local brick-and-mortar retailers because the former didn't have to collect sales tax (unless they had a physical presence in that state), and of states' losing potential tax revenue as more and more items were purchased online. Though this was an issue that had many layers and interests, the resulting statement of purpose was concise and clear:

1. Simplify and make the sales tax better and simpler for multi-state sellers.
2. To take the conclusions to Congress and to obtain legislation that would overturn the Quill decision, which had prohibited collection of the tax for remote sales in the first place.[11]

We supplemented that statement with a series of qualifying points to make clear how this purpose applied in terms of various forms of revenue and tax issues, but the basic purpose was communicated quickly and in a problem-solving manner.

Step Six

Put the purpose in writing and in participants' consciousness.

The purpose must be put in writing in the formal charter rather than merely be a verbal agreement or an unstated understanding (see Chapter Seven). Participants are operating out of self-interest; this is a good thing in the sense that it motivates them to collaborate rather than go it alone, but it also can warp the purpose in their minds. Without a clear statement, they will naturally shade the purpose toward what they and their organizations hope to derive from the collaboration. A written purpose statement avoids this misinterpretation.

In addition, leaders should open every meeting by reiterating the purpose. Even though it may be in the charter, people are unlikely to look at it regularly and remind themselves of exactly what the collaboration is trying to accomplish. By repeating the stated purpose aloud, leaders keep participants focused on it.

Step Seven

Have a process in place to revise or reformulate the purpose.

Ideally, the purpose you put in the charter at the beginning of the collaboration will be viable throughout the group's existence. But circumstances may change. It may be that the pain that motivated people to collaborate has evolved—perhaps what used to be a local problem has become a global one. As a result, the initial purpose needs to be adjusted.

In the initial charter-creating session, then, a provision should be included for revising the purpose if conditions change enough to require it. Still, that initial purpose statement should not be taken lightly or seen as malleable except when major changes occur that clearly show it to be off-target. Again, establish that consensus must be achieved before a purpose can be revised.

THE ART OF PURPOSE

Although the seven-step process will facilitate the framing of a purpose, it is still true that to a certain extent, establishing a clearly defined purpose is an art. This is especially true when conveners and leaders are struggling with articulating the collaboration's reason for existence. In these instances, conveners and leaders should engage participants in a discussion of purpose in the initial session and listen intently to what each participant has to say. What has motivated them to join? How are they feeling the pain? What is driving them? What outcome do they hope for?

This discussion may well require some delicate and inspired negotiation to find a purpose that can achieve consensus from participants. To practice this art, we offer this advice:

Find the golden mean: big enough to matter and small enough to do.

Invariably, participants' varying ideas about purpose will involve scope. Some will favor hugely ambitious objectives while others will insist on small, achievable targets. In most instances, there's a place between ambition and practicality where a viable purpose resides. As a committed leader, you need to develop a sixth sense for when people are setting goals that are too difficult to achieve or too wide-ranging; you also need to grasp when you've shrunk the purpose to the point that its achievement won't have any real impact.

We know that committed leaders have a lot of responsibilities—and that we're adding another one here. Nonetheless, leaders often have the vision and perspective necessary to make the creation of a purpose possible. Once they've helped a number of collaborations create useful purposes, they will also possess the experience and instinct to approach the task with confidence.

SEVEN

A Formal Charter

Framing a purpose is only one part of the groundwork for an effective value alliance. If participants lack common expectations about how the alliance will go about its business, they are unlikely to accomplish anything. Hence the need for a written charter.

A formal charter confers official status on the group and also creates the structure necessary for productivity. A charter can vary in complexity, depending on the situation. A value alliance convened by the leader of an enterprise to organize a collaborative effort among divisions may not need the same level of detail as one initiating an effort to establish common standards among competitors. In both cases, however, a charter serves similar functions, formalizing commitment, agreement about the mission, and key operating parameters.

More important, though, the charter codifies agreement by defining the problem and its scope, the purpose of the collaboration, and the way decisions will be made as the collaboration moves forward. Don't assume that all participants agree on these issues or that any differences will work themselves out naturally as the collaborative effort progresses. In fact, people may be shocked at the range of views participants have on the most basic questions involving the collaboration's scope.

Charter creation is an important job of the convener of stature. After gaining the general agreement of prospective members to participate in a value alliance, good conveners invite all these individuals to a preliminary meeting to make sure everyone is comfortable with each other and the task. If possible, conveners should provide a draft charter. Where competitive tensions exist, conveners can advance agreement quickly by relying on the charter to give all participants an understanding that business will be conducted fairly.

A prerequisite to writing the formal charter is developing a sufficient degree of camaraderie and purpose. Until participants relieve the tension that naturally builds at the beginning of the process, conveners, leaders, and representatives of substance will find it difficult to accept a charter. This tension may be exacerbated when competitors and antagonists gather for their initial meetings. Therefore, it is important to consider all the potential conflicts that can and often do occur in a diverse collaboration:

- Between competitors who don't want to share proprietary information or who feel the collaboration will benefit someone else more than themselves
- Between government groups and businesses that are at loggerheads over an issue
- Between consumer activist groups and business representatives over a social issue
- Between large companies and small ones (or public companies and private ones) that have different cultures and styles of operating
- Between participants who favor fast action and those who prefer a slower pace
- Between participants who are leaders in their own spheres and used to issuing orders rather than working collaboratively

Given the potential tensions, it is incumbent to meet about substantive issues, determine if these tensions are an impediment to progress, and work to resolve them. Cocktail parties and receptions may allow people to get acquainted, but it's only when people with skin in the game sit down at the table and grapple with the common pain and how to relieve it that differences in style, perspective, and personality emerge as tension in the group.

The initial meeting (or a specific session framed around the formal charter) is an ideal setting to deal with these differences, in part because meaningful matters are up for discussion and in part because creating the charter isn't as inherently tension-filled as later discussions on recommended actions will be—the charter topic occupies a middle ground where people can get to know each other and learn to work together on issues related to process rather than on the decisions about implementation that await them. People may push each other a bit, but they generally don't push so hard that someone gets hurt.

Still, creating a charter permits committed leaders to assess the representatives. They observe how people interact, how they facilitate productive and issue-focused discussion, and whether they are inclined to deviate from the topic and lead the group down the road of petty arguments. They may also get their first glimpse of potential cynics, critics, and saboteurs, and have an early opportunity to address their behaviors. When they observe persistent negative and counterproductive behavior, committed leaders may want to ask the prospective participant to leave or at least move off to the side.

Thus the meeting on the charter may reveal things that affect the future of the alliance. It is better to know up front—rather than months down the road—who finds it difficult to get into a collaborative rhythm or who turns issues of principle into discussions that become personal and hostile. More commonly, participants simply need the opportunity to get their feet wet in collaborative waters, and the charter discussion gives them this opportunity. On the positive side, they may be pleasantly surprised by a competitor's ability to listen and compromise or by a government official's willingness to absorb and respond to a CEO's concerns. Ideally, people start developing or solidifying relationships during charter negotiations that will serve the collaboration well later on.

PSYCHOLOGICAL AND MORAL BUY-IN

Collaborative efforts often launch with a period of self-interest. Participants want to express why they're part of the newly formed group in no uncertain terms: *This is the pain we're feeling, this is what we hope to gain from our participation.* Sometimes, participants perseverate about a particular concern of their group, and they can consume large amounts of meeting time focusing on their concerns and insisting they be addressed. Since self-interest is a prime motivator for participation, some of this is to be expected, but there needs to be a moment relatively early on when the participants move past absolute protection of self-interest and start working together toward the common goal.

Creating a formal charter gives participants an opportunity to vent their self-interest and move forward with the greater work of the collaboration. Psychologically, the charter discussion helps people articulate what concerns them most. While self-interest never disappears completely and may even find its way into the language of the charter, it is beneficial to confront and address it up front.

Perhaps as much as anything else, creating and signing a formal charter provides a moral buy-in. In politics and business, the good and noble intentions of possibility can move to the back burner when participants become distracted from their original purpose. The formal charter cements the purpose, creating a moral commitment. The very act of discussing, debating, reducing to writing, and signing off on how the collaboration should operate and what it should strive to achieve enrolls people in the collaboration's mission; it is like signing a pledge, reinforcing the concept that their word is their bond.

Charter documents may have different origins and thus have different names. A value alliance I helped construct in the field of international health is an example. In 2002, AIDS was spreading across the world. Most of the industrialized nations began to offer assistance to underdeveloped countries to fight this disease. However, without a coordinated effort, the process was highly inefficient. A group of nations proposed forming the collaboration that came to be called the Global

Fund, now based in Geneva, Switzerland. The mission of the fund was expanded to provide assistance to treating AIDS, TB, and malaria in 150 countries. Ten years later, donors became uneasy that the fund was not being managed well. In 2011, former President Festus Mohigh of Botswana and I were asked by the Board of Directors of the Global Fund to act as conveners and leaders of a Special High Level Panel to review the fund's operations and to provide specific recommendations. As co-chairmen, President Mohigh and I negotiated a charter-like document with the Board of the Global Fund, which was referred to as the "Terms of Reference." The Terms of Reference was our charter. The document spelled out a specific set of tasks and accountabilities. Even more valuably, it created a psychological and moral buy-in that ensured full and committed participation.

THE ESSENTIAL INGREDIENTS

Charters function like a combination of bylaws and operating plan. There is no magic format. In some cases charters are negotiated between parties for weeks. Others amount to quick documents drafted among peers.

The Western Regional Air Partnership (WRAP) evolved from an earlier collaboration, the Grand Canyon Visibility Transport Commission, a collaboration of federal, state, and local governments, Indian tribes, businesses, and others. WRAP was created to implement a solution to the problem of pollution in the air over the Grand Canyon. We've included parts of the charter here (see the Appendix for full charter) to give you a sense of the types of issues it covers. It's divided into three sections: Purposes, Principles, and Operating Procedures. The Purposes section defines the scope of WRAP in the form of nine statements, including "Develop a common understanding of current and evolving regional air quality issues in the West." Principles, which is the shortest section in the charter, recognizes the limits of the partnership's responsibility and notes the federal government's responsibility to protect tribal resources. And Operating Procedures covers a wide range of issues, from how decisions will be made to the powers of the WRAP board of directors.[1]

Instead of reviewing every part of the charter, this chapter focuses on the crucial parts, the ones that play the most significant role in helping create a value alliance.

First, the Purpose section helps participants set parameters for its work. It may seem obvious why a collaboration was formed, but in many instances, participants have different ideas about how to solve the problem it faces, how the problem should be defined, or what other problems might be included in their efforts. For instance, we noted that one purpose in the WRAP charter was "understanding . . . evolving air quality issues in the West." Thus, the scope was defined more broadly than it might have been, in part because pollution in areas relatively far from the Grand Canyon could still affect air quality above it.

Second, the Principles section gives participants a chance to discuss the larger values and concerns behind their upcoming work. In the WRAP charter, this section expressed sensitivity to tribal lands and peoples, and acknowledging this principle meant that it had to be considered when making any decision. Expressing higher-level beliefs and values gives the formal charter moral weight—it's not just a document of procedures but one of principles.

Third, the Operating Procedures section sets out some practical basics. It is where a collaboration structure becomes very helpful in helping alliance members deal with conflicts and impasses that might otherwise stymie their efforts.

The details of a formal charter may seem simple, but getting these basics right will provide a strong foundation for an alliance as it moves forward. Here are the matters a charter must address as well as why they're important:

Who the members will be: The composition of the alliance can be a challenge to articulate. In most cases the convener will have assembled the group. However, it is not unusual to discover that a perspective is missing or for a new player to ask for inclusion. Still, an effort must be made to identify a diverse and complete group of representatives.

Who the leaders will be or how they will be chosen: As discussed in Chapter Five, in the majority of collaborations, a convener appoints the leader. However, in other instances, a group may select its own leader.

In those cases, having a selection process is critical for the chemistry of the alliance and can help avoid the damage of a contentious election.

How meetings will be called: In most cases this is fairly straightforward in that the participants arrange meetings to fit their collective schedules. In some settings, though, public notice is important (for instance, when transparency is a requirement).

How decisions will be made: The fundamental question here is whether to seek consensus, use simple voting, or apply formal rules of order. I have found that consensus rules work best in value alliances. A consensus democracy functions much differently from a majority-rules process. In a majority-rules process, the presumption is that all the participants will be subject to the majority. In a value alliance, the presumption is that participants are there voluntarily acting on self-interest, and if they ever get to the point of feeling they would be better off outside the process, they can (and will) leave. In a majority vote system, the primary goal is a decision. In a value alliance, the objective is a broad agreement on mutual benefit. A consensus-based process typically drives broader participation among the group because everyone's opinion becomes both important and necessary. Listening enjoys a new prominence as participants try to learn the concerns and perspectives of the other participants; simple majority discussions typically aren't as inclusive. Consensus rules allow flexibility until a critical mass finds comfort and typically drives this deeper effort to understand what everyone is trying to communicate. (We've included this pro-consensus summary here to help you make this argument during formal charter discussions.)

How to make financial arrangements: Collaborative efforts may require money for staffing, research, and other needs; in some instances, direct investment is necessary. Meanwhile, representatives may feel uncertain and even awkward about specifying who will meet these needs. This is true even if the value alliance involves different departments within the same company. When fundraising to sustain a value alliance over time is required, the charter should be explicit in assigning responsibility with deadlines. Making the arrangements up front and putting them in writing helps participants face reality squarely.

What time frames are relevant: Time expectations often determine the attractiveness of a value alliance. They can also create conflict among collaborative teams. While charters are dynamic documents, sketching time-related milestones into the charter along with a description of how the group will track progress are key initial steps. Typically we attach a list of milestones and commit in the charter that an updated version will be circulated periodically. The beginning report from the One Page Project Management (OPPM) system, introduced in Chapter Eight, serves admirably for this exercise, creating the necessary urgency to move forward.[2]

Deadlines can drive discussions and create action. If deadlines are unrealistic, however, they can be counterproductive, producing the perception of failure. And if deadlines are too generous, then the charter will encourage a great deal of self-interested talk and very little action. So it's important to try to be as objective and accurate as possible in this charter task.

The Grand Canyon Visibility Transport Commission had a five-year deadline, and the first four years featured participants' arguing for their own preferred solutions to the problem and a tacit refusal to find common ground and take action. It was only during the last year of the collaboration, when the deadline was looming, that people overcame their own self-interest, reached consensus, and found and implemented a solution to the pollution problem. If the charter had specified a tighter deadline, it might have helped the group arrive at a solution much earlier.

Who is responsible for what tasks: Value alliances need accountability. Typically, the person or entity to whom they report is the convener. Accountability is enhanced when the charter lays out clear deliverables and deadlines.

Ideally, charters will specify a series of intermediate deadlines tied to actions—get x done by one date, get y done by another date—leading up to a deadline for reaching a larger, problem-solving goal. This creates milestones for participants to measure their progress and also confers momentum on the collaboration as one milestone after another is achieved.

How members share information: When competitors collaborate to find mutual advantage, they often need to disclose sensitive or confidential information. For example, if a group of businesses began discussing the formation of an alliance under which they would collaboratively share the use of certain assets, it might be necessary to have information about customers and current protocols used. Parties should anticipate this and agree in advance rather than getting to an advanced point in the work only to discover that one of the key players views the information as proprietary and refuses to disclose it.

At the other end of the scale, information sharing and cooperation can trigger worries about anticompetitive behavior. I have been involved in several alliances where collaborative arrangements had to be analyzed by lawyers with this concern in mind.

What level of confidentiality is acceptable: Confidentiality should be dealt with in two ways. First, establish the degree to which specific information can be disclosed by participants. At times, information about the mere existence of a value alliance may create market sensitivities, or specific information generated in the course of the effort may have proprietary importance. Second, in alliances where a public interest is involved, the charter should specify who is authorized to speak on behalf of the alliance (to make sure that sensitive information isn't disclosed prematurely or conveyed in a way that causes unnecessary alarm).

How to amend a charter: Situations often change, rendering charter-ratified details out of date or just plain wrong. Because charters are a combination of bylaws and operating plan, they have to be considered dynamic documents, easily alterable by agreement of the participants. For this reason, then, a process for amending the charter must be discussed and embedded in the charter. Again, it is important to remember that consensus-based organizations operate differently from majority-rule entities. If the group can agree to amend its charter, according to its collaborative rules, then it should. An inherent check-and-balance system is in place—if participants begin to feel disadvantaged by amendments to the charter, they will leave, potentially reducing the benefit to the other participants.

A CHARTER EXAMPLE

Charters vary quite a bit in their language and style. To help you recognize the differences—and to encourage you to tailor your charter to the particular sensibilities of your representatives and their concerns—here are two purpose sections from charters. First, this is the purpose statement from the Great Lakes Regional Collaboration:[3]

> The purpose of this Framework is to establish the Great Lakes Regional Collaboration to enhance the U.S. efforts to restore and protect the Great Lakes ecosystem. . . . The Strategy Teams will operate by a consensus process that parallels the process described in Section V.A. The Strategy Team Chairs will be the Presiders of the Strategy Team meetings and will be responsible for determining when a consensus has or has not been reached.

Compare that with the following excerpt from the Performance Monitoring and Evaluation section of the GEOSS charter:[4]

> The purpose of GEOSS is to achieve comprehensive, coordinated and sustained observations of the Earth system, in order to improve monitoring of the state of the Earth, increase understanding of Earth processes, and enhance prediction of the behavior of the Earth system. The benefits to society have been initially categorized into nine areas:
>
> - Reducing loss of life and property from natural and human-induced disasters
> - Understanding environmental factors affecting human health and well being
> - Improving management of energy resources
> - Understanding, assessing, predicting, mitigating, and adapting to climate variability and change

- Improving water resource management through better understanding of the water cycle
- Improving weather information, forecasting, and warning
- Improving the management and protection of terrestrial, coastal, and marine ecosystems
- Supporting sustainable agriculture and combating desertification
- Understanding, monitoring, and conserving biodiversity

As you can see, these two charter sections reflect the specific issues and approaches of their respective groups. You should create a charter that reflects the style and substance of your alliance (rather than using language that feels uncomfortable or may be off-putting to participants).

Despite the differences in style and substance among purpose statements, they should address many common factors. To give you a quick look at these factors, Table 7.1 presents a comparison chart involving three purpose statements. As you look at this chart, you'll see that one statement may have omitted dealing with the issue of charter amendments while another failed to address consensus decision-making. A charter is still valid and useful even with a few omissions. Sufficient dialogue must exist to create a working charter. Producing an overly short and simplistic charter ignores many critical issues. Charters aren't just for show. Instead, they provide the reassurance of a comprehensive, formal document that both guides the group and reinforces members' sense of mission.

SIGNING THE CHARTER

Charters should be signed by every participant. Signing connotes agreement to abide by the charter's terms. If only the leader or the convener signs, the alliance misses an opportunity to create buy-in. Psychologically as well as substantively, the act of signing this document is beneficial.

Charter signing can also create the feeling of a strong beginning. Chapter Three describes a "flags and bagpipe meeting" where a charter signing was celebrated as the launching pad for significant

Table 7.1 Formal Charter Cross Examination

Element	GEOSS	WRAP	GLRC
Purpose and Goals	✓	✓	✓
Principles and Overview	✓	✓	✓
Operating Procedures	✓	✓	✓
Membership and Participation	✓	✓	✓
Roles, Responsibilities, and Powers	✓	✓	✓
Board of Directors and Executive Committee	✓	✓	✓
Meetings	✓	✓	✓
Consensus and Issue Resolution		✓	✓
Charter Amendments		✓	
Road Map and Timetable	✓		✓
Monitoring and Evaluation	✓		

accomplishment. Some value alliances derive an important public benefit from this kind of meeting. In those cases, a well-executed signing ceremony with media coverage of handshakes, speeches, and other ceremonial elements provides a show of progress reporters can write about.

In most cases, though, charter signings benefit representatives the most. They are the ones who are energized by the signing and can draw on it in the days ahead.

EIGHT

The Northbound Train

Of all the eight elements of a value alliance, the northbound train is the least tangible. Yet in many ways, it is one of the most critical. That's because collaborations are voluntary enterprises operating with presumed authority. People can leave the collaboration at any time; they can also remain as participants yet cut back on the time, effort, or resources they're willing to devote to it. When a critical mass of participants leave a voluntary alliance, the effort fails. A committed leader, no matter how skilled or influential, will struggle to hold the collaboration together when members perceive it to be dead in the water or making imperceptible progress.

People want to invest their time, money, and reputation on things that will make a difference. The phrase "northbound train" is shorthand for "Decisions that matter to me are going to be made and I need to be there. The train is headed north and I want a seat on it."

A POLITICAL TRAIN HEADING NORTH

In May 2012 I had a conversation with former Governor Mitt Romney, who at that time was seeking the Republican nomination for president. Governor Romney and I have a long-held friendship and working relationship that started in 1998 when I asked him to lead the 2002 Winter

Olympic Games in Utah. This time, Governor Romney had a request for me. He had just won a series of state primary elections and his principal opponents had withdrawn from the race. He said, "It looks like we may win the nomination. However, I didn't run to just get the nomination—I ran to make some serious changes in the direction of our country. If we win, we will have only seventy-seven days until the inauguration and that isn't enough time to prepare. I would like you to convene a group to quietly get ready to govern."

Over the next six months, the country watched the very public campaign between President Obama and Governor Romney. What they didn't see was the collaborative entity Governor Romney and I developed: the Readiness Project. This was massive value alliance designed to organize a transition of administrations should Governor Romney win the general election. While every presidential nominee prepares in a similar way, these efforts must be undertaken below the public radar. Otherwise, they could become a distraction to the campaign.

The Readiness Project had these major deliverables: Put a team on the field quickly (staffing the White House, the Cabinet, and the top 150 senior executive positions); develop a detailed plan for the first two hundred days; write a federal budget; organize all the necessary functions of a White House in waiting; coordinate all this with Congress. Every one of the deliverables required extensive collaborative work.

Our approach was to create miniature version of the executive branch of the U.S. government. As Election Day approached, you could walk down the halls of the 120,000-square-foot federal building we occupied in Washington D.C. and find nearly six hundred people (mostly volunteers) organized into more than seventy separate teams representing the different parts of the federal government. These were highly trained and experienced professionals, experts in specific fields of policy. Most of them had served in senior executive roles in previous administrations or in Congress. As we prepared for the first two hundred days of a new administration, teams worked to prepare the executive orders and rule-making actions needed to implement the agenda Governor Romney had proposed. Each of these required the formation of a task force designed to replicate the interagency process used in the White House to reconcile the conflicting perspectives among different parts of the government.

Our effort was a laboratory for collaboration, and as a value alliance, it highlights the value of maintaining the perception of a northbound train. As the Readiness Project quietly organized, the fortunes of the presidential campaign fluctuated. There were times during the late summer and early fall that polls were not encouraging. During those periods the leadership of the Readiness Project had to work hard at keeping the volunteers in the organization focused and motivated.

On October 3, 2012, the first presidential debate occurred in Denver, and Governor Romney scored a resounding victory, creating a momentum shift. The next morning contributions poured into the campaign coffers and simultaneously the Readiness Project became a cool place in Washington D.C. People began to volunteer in droves—vying to get a seat on the northbound train. Those who had a seat on the train were energized. Suddenly, it appeared a Romney presidency could happen and people wanted to be part of it.

All three of the basic motivations outlined in Chapter Two manifested themselves as people joined the effort for a variety of reasons. The notions of greed, fear, and touching the hand of greatness may seem a bit bare-knuckled when used in the context of friends and colleagues, but the concepts create context even if they are articulated as nobility, selflessness, and a basic sense of responsibility. *Greed* made people want to board the train because it might provide a job opportunity in the new administration or an opportunity to affect policies of the new administration. *Fear* warned that policy decisions were going to be made that could alter participants' organizations or lives, and it would be better to affect them now than fight them later. And the desire to *touch the hand of greatness* manifested in a wish to be close to the center and participate in events that could shape the country.

We vetted participants to make sure that the last motivation was evident and that they possessed the integrity and loyalty to prevent them from acting solely out of the first one. Still, these participants—like participants in any value alliance—had a mix of motivations, a mix that keeps people on board until the alliance has accomplished its mission or until the final vote is in.

WHEN A NORTHBOUND TRAIN
BEGINS TO SLOW

Every value alliance has a brand in the community of interest it serves. That brand is shaped by the degree to which people believe the alliance is a northbound train, likely to reach an important destination. The quality of the brand is greatly affected by the degree of common pain, the strength of the convener and leader, and their skill in creating and communicating momentum. At the same time, conveners and committed leaders need to recognize when that brand is being diminished in any way. Typically in a value alliance, this happens when the northbound train begins to lose momentum. In these instances, it is essential to recognize that it is decelerating and know what to do about it.

What can stall, even kill momentum? In short: Failure to meet expectations. Participants join collaborations with certain assumptions about how the group will solve a problem, how quickly it will solve it, and who will provide the resources and take responsibility for specific problem-solving tasks. When their expectations about these and other developments aren't met, they perceive that the collaboration has lost something—its momentum, its raison d'être, its mandate. Sometimes, participants can point to a particular metric as emblematic of the coalition's southbound state—a beta test that failed, for instance. In other situations, it's less tangible—a waning of enthusiasm from both the leader and participants. Whatever causes this perceived stall in momentum, it robs the collaboration of energy and sense of mission, and it often spells the beginning of the end if the northbound perception isn't restored.

Identifying loss of momentum is the first step. Here are some relatively common warning signs:

• *Diminishing attendance.* Participants may begin attending meetings sporadically, ceasing to attend at all, or sending lower-level people in their place. Whatever form this takes, it tells other participants that those who are absent or attending less frequently believe the collaboration is less important than they once thought. An empty seat sends an unmistakable message, especially when it's empty consistently. Similarly, when important principal players send stand-ins to fill their chairs, it can often mean the effort has slipped as a priority.

Solution: The convener or leader has to talk to absentee principals about their lack of participation. This is a situation when the leader has to play the role of counselor or disciplinarian.

• *Stalemates.* While vigorous debate often highlights a value alliance's vitality, debate that degenerates into feuding is another matter entirely. Dangerous disputes are loud, hostile, repeated (at one meeting after another), and personal, and they never seem to be resolved. These frequent battles get on people's nerves, but more significantly, they suggest a stalemate—that there is a divide in the collaboration that is preventing the group from taking action. Others in the group quickly sense a problem that will never be resolved and begin tuning out. Deeply ingrained stalemates are not just momentum killers but value alliance killers. This is especially true if the unsolved tension is between two parties critical to the outcome. Stalemates may also have their roots in historical competitive pressures where two individuals choose to act out their frustrations.

Solution: To deal with momentum-killing stalemates, you have two options: First, suspend the balance of activities on the agenda so that people don't feel their time is being wasted (and lose trust in a positive outcome because of the stalemate). Second, gain agreement among the collaborative players to move forward on other parts of the task while the leader and those involved in the dispute settle on a solution.

During my time as secretary of HHS, we worked collaboratively to build a system of advanced laboratories around the world. The system required countries where new infectious influenza viruses appeared to send a sample to one of these advanced laboratories so that a vaccine could be made to combat it. A couple of small countries saw this as an opportunity to create leverage in an old fight about access to free vaccines. We spent a significant amount of time trying to resolve it, and our collaborative efforts were stalled by this tactic. Ultimately, we minimized the impact of the disruption by proceeding without the protesting parties. They had power only so long as we allowed them to disrupt our work. Getting the collaborative network built took precedence over full participation. So even though the alliance was diminished somewhat when a handful of countries didn't participate, we pressed on, maintaining our momentum.

• *Inability to meet timetables or metrics.* In a value alliance, the perception of progress is subjective and tied to the expectations of the participants. Varying expectations mean at least one participant is likely to be disappointed by how quickly the alliance is moving or what it has achieved to date.

Solution: Formal agreement on time lines is imperative. We have adopted a commercially available system known as One Page Project Manager to help in driving all the collaborative projects we do. One Page breaks down the critical path to success and devises a time line for each step. It also designates responsibility for delivering each component and the associated time commitments. By agreeing in advance on this system and keeping participants aware of the time line, alliances can avert problems or deal with them effectively.

• *An unexpected event.* A participant may withdraw from the collaboration, taking critical resources away; or the collaboration may test a possible solution in a particular location or area and it fails; or the committed leader may depart or cut back for any number of reasons (health, regular job requirements, or whatever); or a major technological, social, or economic change may ease the common pain and rob the collaboration of its catalyst. While this last event is greeted positively by the collaboration even as it disbands, the other events can devastate the morale of participants and send a northbound train off the tracks.

Solution: When changes impinge on a collaboration, the leader has two duties. First, recalibrate the entire value equation to determine if the opportunity foreseen by the convener still exists. Second, communicate the implications of the impact to participants and in so doing reset expectations.

• *Alternative approaches surface.* For instance, participants (or nonparticipants) signal their discontent with a collaborative process by establishing alternative or competing alliances. Typically, a splinter group from the collaboration breaks off and forms its own group. The departing participants may be a minority with a different point of view on the problem or they may want to pursue a solution more aggressively (or less so). When they break off and start working on solving the same problem as the larger collaborative group, they raise doubts—are they pursuing the right strategy to solve the problem and are we pursuing the wrong one? Their existence also gives other participants the option of deserting the older collaborative group for the newer one. In either case, this alternative approach may create the impression that the train is going in the wrong direction or at the wrong speed.

Solution: Recognize that a splinter group is a warning sign, revealing significant discontent. In value alliances seeking to establish a best practice or standard, it means that failure has occurred. The leader and convener must meet with the discontented groups and try to unify the effort again. The best way to do so is to remind the discontented that their pain is common and that unless a harmonized solution is arrived at, little relief will occur. An exception to this rule involves businesses using collaborative approaches to create joint venture teams to compete for a project. In these cases, if reconciliation is not achieved, the best course is for alternative partners to take over the task.

• *Scope creep.* Expanding the mission of a group, generally to satisfy the desires of a minority of participants, nearly always leads to trouble, as with the attempt to turn a high school track and field facility development into a world-class track center described in Chapter Six. This kind of dangerous redefinition affects both big and small projects and collaborations. Members can become so excited about all the resources they've gathered collaboratively that they believe they can accomplish much more than they set out to, and so they make their group's plans more ambitious than they should be. The complexities and costs associated with this broadening of scope change the way people view the collaboration for the worse.

Solution: Define an achievable scope early. The leader should make sure it's written into the group's charter document. Then both the convener and the leader must resist opportunities to expand it.

In the Readiness Project, I made an early decision that we would limit the scope of our work to the commitments Governor Romney had made in his campaign. As you can imagine, many people wanted to expand the work of this group to incorporate other issues important to them. In past transition-planning efforts, this type of scope creep had been allowed. The result: large binders containing so many initiatives the incoming department head couldn't begin to respond to all of them—so they were ignored. This is a sure way to put the brakes on a northbound train. We wrote very explicit charters for each function, and as chairman, I was the only one who could expand a charter.

IT'S OK TO FAIL—JUST DO IT EARLY

Not every value alliance succeeds. Sometimes they fail because the common pain wasn't as intense as it initially seemed. It's also possible that the solution proposed or implemented by the alliance turned out to be more painful than the problem. On occasion, the situation will change and a critical mass of participants suddenly lose their motivation. Or the participants in the collaboration become focused on a higher-priority issue and lose track of the one that brought them together.

Whatever the cause of failure, leaders and conveners may want to test the group's willingness to continue. Value alliances operate like parliamentary governments. If a majority ever loses confidence in its leadership, the effort can disband. Alliance leaders must determine if and when that point has been reached. Allowing alliances to linger too long after they have clearly lost their momentum only prolongs the inevitable and damages the reputation of the convener. If you are going to fail, fail early.

CREATING THE PERCEPTION OF A NORTHBOUND TRAIN

No doubt, you've seen CEOs and political leaders who were brilliant at creating the perception of a northbound train. President Ronald Reagan and General Electric's Jack Welch projected such great confidence in their enterprises, their people, and the future that they convinced many people that the country and company were going in the right direction. Certain professional sports coaches, too, are able to attract free agents and instill confidence in their teams, their fans, and their ownership because they are skilled at generating positive perceptions.

What these leaders have in common is an ability to motivate people in large groups or in one-on-one conversations. They're often savvy about how to use media—both new media and old—and they generally possess a certain charisma that contributes to the positive perceptions they create.

While committed leaders may not have the same positional advantages as high-profile figures in industry or government, they can create the perception of a northbound train by doing the following:

- *Hold ratifying events.* Committed leaders capitalize on the validating effect of conferences, keynote addresses, and other formal occasions. Collaborations often need an event to communicate their substance and purpose to participants, who have little prior experience with them. These events allow leaders to create esprit de corps as well as officially announce plans, milestones, and successes. The Surescripts launch conference, for example, helped John Driscoll and Bruce Roberts convince participants that fierce competitors could work together for the common good.
- *Give pep talks.* These can take the form of public addresses to all participants or one-on-one dialogues. Committed leaders and conveners have the power to create a perception of success; their words take on greater weight because of their stature. Participants also play an important role in maintaining momentum—or stalling it. In some instances, a participant who turns into an active cynic can discourage other members

of the group and can start to turn the train south. When the criticism escalates beyond mere cynicism to active levels of disruption, leaders need to take control and convince these naysayers that their efforts jeopardize the alliance. There are times, too, when committed leaders should deliver a motivational talk to all participants, sharing their vision and reminding participants how the collaboration can achieve great things or solve their problems.

• *Provide updates.* The way committed leaders communicate can play a significant role in keeping participants involved and excited about the collaboration. Updates can convey a range of information—tasks assigned and completed, developments in the outside world that affect the collaboration's objectives, small but significant achievements (new participants, funding received, plans tested, and so on). Information can and should be shared at regular meetings and also through more formal means—e-mail, website posts, and the like. Information forms the glue of the collaboration—the more informed participants are about progress being made, the more positive they are likely to be about the group's prospects for solving a problem.

• *Use the media.* Conveners and committed leaders can create external perceptions that influence the perception of the collaborators. Traditionally, the way to do this was to generate an article in a prominent publication or appear on a national talk show—and sometimes the publicity did buoy collaborators; rightly or wrongly, the media's stamp of approval signified that the outside world viewed their efforts as valid. Now, blogs and other new media tools offer leaders an additional method to create buzz for the collaborative effort—ideally, viral buzz that spreads through social media.

• *Promote full participation.* When everyone who should be on board joins or commits, participants feel they are part of something big moving toward a destination. In the IFTA (International Fuel Tax Agreement) collaboration, participants were enthused about the effort in part because all forty-eight contiguous states were involved. The government had provided a powerful incentive: If states didn't participate in IFTA, they would not be able to collect fuel tax from truck companies crossing their states. This brought in states such as Virginia and New Jersey that had resisted joining initially because they felt private bodies such as IFTA lacked the authority to collect the fuel tax. Once the government indicated that IFTA could collect it and that those outside IFTA could not, all the states participated—and this full participation made everyone feel that success was inevitable.[1]

SIGNS OF A NORTHBOUND TRAIN

You can monitor your progress toward creating a northbound train through tangible and intangible means. From a tangible standpoint, assess and determine that you're receiving the resources necessary for the alliance to solve the problem it faces—resources that range from money to equipment to facilities. If your resource levels are at least adequate and at best abundant over a sustained period, then it's likely that the alliance has momentum on its side.

Beyond resources, the train is moving full steam ahead when people are volunteering to join up or offering other types of assistance. Influential individuals call you and ask what they can do to help; participants show up at all collaborative meetings and are fully engaged in contributing ideas and suggesting direction.

Less tangibly, there's a clear sense of purpose and optimism surrounding the alliance. Representatives are upbeat and energized. Conversations are not about if the alliance can succeed but when and to what extent. There's a buzz in the air that conveys the importance of the alliance and the pride people take in participating.

This sense of a northbound train is a hallmark of a value alliance, and it's what can sustain the collaboration over the rough patches and provide the momentum to implement its problem-solving plan. While all eight elements contribute to holding the group together, the feeling generated by a northbound train is what carries the collaboration to its destination.

NINE

Defining Common Ground

Defining common ground, the eighth and final element of a value alliance, is often a predictor of success. To function effectively, the parties need to develop trust in each other and the processes that govern them. Achieving trust requires an unusual degree of transparency as the parties determine the underlying assumptions, sources of information, and standards upon which they will rely. Effective collaboration requires that these be part of a common information base, permitting everyone the chance to operate with the same information. This points, once again, to the difference between advocacy, where parties may keep vital information close to the vest to advance a cause, and consensus, where the parties openly share information in pursuit of a common solution.

All three terms—assumptions, sources, and standards—address complex issues that can make all the difference to the success of a value alliance.

COMMON ASSUMPTIONS

Participants and leaders need to discuss the beliefs and ideas that they take for granted in their collaborative efforts. In the business world, the first budgeting step is to agree on how much money will be available. This often depends on a series of assumptions about future sales results, inflation rates, and what others will do in the market. Because most assumptions involve speculative outcomes, they are subjective judgments. However, assumptions shape the budgeting logic.

In public service roles, I learned the importance of establishing core assumptions early on in a project or process. As head of the Environmental Protection Agency, I had to agree to new regulations. A diverse group of experts with varying perspectives from within the agency would develop the proposed rule and present and defend their work. It worked much like an appeals court. I was given a written briefing to study beforehand. The team would then summarize the matter verbally and explain the impact the new regulation would have.

These matters often dealt with the amount of a particular pollutant the EPA would tolerate being released into the air, water, or soil. Generally, the standard was measured in parts (molecules, for example) per million or billion. The EPA's task was to forecast the impact an accumulation greater than the standard would have on human health.

At the outset, the key was agreement on core assumptions regarding the pollutant and its impact. During discussions at EPA meetings, someone (generally a scientist) would communicate the basis for the conclusions. The discussion included the process the scientist employed to arrive at the conclusions; the models a scientist used required assumptions. The level of tolerable pollution would then be plugged into another complicated economic model (also dependent on assumptions driven by subjective judgments) to determine the cost. I would ask to see the results of the model using a different set of assumptions.

I realized conclusions about the future are driven by assumptions, and assumptions are open to challenge by reasonable people. In the consensus decision-making model that operates in most value alliances, participants must seek agreement right away on assumptions related to the problem. If they fail to do so, conflict will arise later on as recommendations are made and actions are taken. For instance, suppose an alliance is convened to deal with pollution in a community. The representatives include consumer activist groups, companies that pollute, government agencies, and so on. Some representatives assume that their mission is to eliminate 100 percent of the pollution in five years; others believe their goal is to reduce pollution by 75 percent over a longer period of time; and still others assume that any small reduction in pollution within a ten-year time frame would be sufficient. Obviously, unless assumptions are articulated, debated, and agreed upon from the start, no outcome will be satisfactory to a significant percentage of the participants.

Recognize that assumptions are not always quantitative. People also make qualitative assumptions about what constitutes success or failure. In the pollution control example, it may be that one representative of a large corporation believes success is a decrease in the number of negative media stories about that industry, while the consumer activist representative believes success is creating a new entity that constantly monitors pollution levels. Absent discussion and agreement early in the process, the likelihood of success is diminished significantly.

COMMON STANDARDS

Standards aspire to harmonize practices by specifying a right way to do a particular thing. Confusion exists when there are multiple standards or ways to do things. This confusion manifested itself during the discussions about medical records when a perceptive participant said the beautiful thing about standards in the medical record industry is that there are so many to choose from. Common standards were precisely the issue that required attention early in the alliance discussions regarding greater interoperability in electronic medical records. One early project required coordination of lab test results being transferred between electronic medical record (EMR) systems built by different vendors. While most EMR systems have the ability to deliver test results internally, few had interoperability between systems. Without this ability, the second doctor in a different medical system often repeats a patient laboratory test, doubling the expense.

Over time, a group of mostly nonprofit collaborative organizations have been organized within the health care space to standardize the way business processes are conducted. These are called standards development organizations (SDOs). One of those organizations, the Regenstrief Institute, in 1994 began overseeing the electronic reporting of lab test results. The standard is titled Logical Observation Identifiers Names and Codes (LOINC). Most internal transfer of information within an EMR system follows LOINC. The problem of transferring data between systems was complicated by two issues. First, most vendors modified LOINC to some extent to meet their own preferences. Second, other standards interact with LOINC within a system.[1] For example, a standard called SNOMED defines the standard meaning of medical terms, and another called HL7 defines device interoperability standards. Once again, because medical record vendors had modified these standards for their own use, it was difficult for the computer systems to talk with each other.[2]

Each standard had devoted disciples who supported it with great fervor. In each case, the nonprofit alliance existed to govern the process of constant refinement and make an effort to harmonize electronic medical record system developers who had used these standards in slightly different ways.

COMMON SOURCES AND A COMMON BASE OF INFORMATION

Until agreement is reached on authoritative sources of information and expertise, success in a value alliance is hard to achieve. Equally important is the requirement to make all information available to all participants in a transparent and an easily accessible way.

A good example of common sources can be drawn from the Grand Canyon Visibility Transport Commission. In devising a plan to clean the air, different interests found advantage in disputing the impact of specific proposals. They would do so by producing a study from an impressive group or person backing their claim—many times in direct contradiction of another respected source.

Scientific evidence is rarely absolute and is often subject to significant variation in opinion. An important question we have learned to ask is, "Whose science?" Scientific evidence is valuable because it is based on a methodical approach to exploration. But competent scientists often disagree. Therefore, alliance members must agree on common sources of scientific advice in the beginning; without that, competing interests will eventually divide the alliance. This does not preclude adding additional information later, as long as it's only added with the agreement of the participants.

Resolving issues related to assumptions, standards, or sources tests the resilience of the value alliance. For example, will an electronic medical record vendor who has a lab test reporting system try to find a solution as part of a collaboration even though the solution may require changes to that system? Or will this vendor become a saboteur, believing that it's better to undercut the alliance than to have to alter the system? Similarly, will an energy company that contributes to the pollution problem over the Grand Canyon support a solution based on analysis (a common source) it doesn't control or will it withdraw its support?

The answers to these questions depend on whether the representatives involved are experiencing sufficient common pain to keep them participating. Ideally, alliances will recognize that they need to address all these questions at the beginning of the collaborative process and arrive at uniform assumptions, standards, and sources and basic information.

The Global Earth Observation System of Systems (GEOSS) provides a compelling argument for standards and an information base. As noted, GEOSS is an extremely diverse international collaboration designed to monitor environmental changes throughout the world. Without common standards and information protocols, the collaboration would quickly dissolve; some countries would feel left out of the loop while others would believe their observations weren't being taken seriously. To avoid these outcomes, the alliance set up the GEOSS Portal for members to exchange data freely and openly. In fact, free and open data dissemination has been a fundamental principle of GEOSS from the beginning.

Initially, this type of common-information principle may draw protest from participants with strong views about proprietary information. India, for instance, did not want to participate in GEOSS at first because of national security issues—Indian representatives didn't want to share their country's information with countries that might be hostile to it. They quickly realized, however, that the common pain of environmental pollution needed to be addressed, and that they could address it more effectively if they had access to the observation systems provided by other countries. Despite reservations about revealing sensitive information, India grasped that having access to a common information base was a worthwhile trade-off and therefore agreed to participate in GEOSS.

When a convener and committed leader identify common linchpin issues involving assumptions, standards, and sources and resolve them early, the chances of alliance success increase dramatically. Among other advantages, such early resolution is a strong indication that participants are willing to work collaboratively to solve problems.

Creating these commonalities isn't just a way to avoid negative outcomes—it sets the alliance up to achieve positive ones. In fact, the more agreements collaborators can reach in advance, the more successful the collaboration will be. Each commonality provides another strand that binds a diverse group of people and organizations together. When participants have reached agreement about the research they'll rely on, the way new developments and other news will be distributed to members, and the terms they'll use to refer to key concepts and groups within the collaboration, they will have strengthened the group immeasurably.

MITIGATING DISAGREEMENT

When an alliance cannot reach consensus or near consensus on a critical assumption, source, or standard, the leader must find a way to move the alliance forward. Sustaining a value alliance is similar to riding a bicycle. If you lose momentum it will begin to wobble and ultimately tip over. When disagreement exists over assumptions, sources, or standards, momentum diminishes. If this lack of commonality isn't addressed, the alliance will probably topple.

Leaders can help regain momentum in a number of ways. First and foremost, they should remind participants that nothing is agreed to until everything is agreed to. New ways of resolving a lack of commonality about assumptions, standards, and sources may appear. Here are some techniques we have used to regain momentum in the face of disagreement:

Operate on a non-consensus majority: In the absence of consensus or near consensus, the leader can simply move forward (rather than stay mired in momentum-killing disagreement). Acknowledge the objection of dissenters, making it clear to them that the alliance can revisit the issue as new ideas or options come on the table. While dissenters may accept this plan and allow the alliance to move forward, they may also choose to withdraw from participation. If that occurs, the convener must determine whether the objective of the value alliance can still be met without them.

Allow the convener or another trusted third party to decide: In situations where the alliance is divided among multiple options, the leader can propose that the convener be asked to make a decision, thus enabling the work to go forward.

Put together a blended decision: Sometimes it is possible to integrate input from differing participants to achieve acceptable assumptions, standards, and sources. In an international collaborative exercise, our alliance was debating the language our work would be conducted in. We resolved the matter by arranging simultaneous interpretation. It required additional money but it allowed our work to go forward. In other alliances involving disputes related to quantitative measures that will be the standards, one solution that can work is agreeing to use an average measure (one that blends the two quantitative measures in dispute).

Operate in a range: This means that you regain momentum by agreeing a range of acceptable standards with an understanding that a more precise decision will have to be made in the future. Many times, as the alliance evolves, new options become available or the dispute becomes less important. Essentially, participants agree that they'll keep an open mind regarding a standard, for instance, and they tolerate activities that aren't locked into one particular standard.

Hold a focused session to reengineer the problem: Sometimes, representatives disagree about an assumption, standard, or source because of misunderstanding or bias. Leaders can bring the disagreeing parties together in a separate session and examine why the assumption, source, or standard is important to each representative. Then leaders can focus the discussion on whether bias or a lack of communication or knowledge has created an impasse. Digging into the details of misunderstanding and bias can sometimes help participants find common ground. Through a facilitated discussion, people can view the problem differently and understand it better or they can recognize how their unconscious bias is causing them to resist agreement on commonalities.

Strike a grand bargain: Here the leader's strategy is to foster agreement by finding a way to reposition an assumption, standard, or source so that it makes concessions to both sides in a dispute. When each side gets something they want, it is easier for them to accept something they initially didn't want.

TWO TECHNIQUES TO FOSTER COMMON UNDERSTANDING

Beyond using mitigation tactics, leaders and conveners can be proactive in their approach to the issue of assumptions, standards, and sources. In some instances, they can create common ground among representatives by focusing on two over-arching subjects:

- Principles
- Information gathering and dissemination

Principles

The process of gaining consensus on principles helps ensure that representatives are on the same page when it comes to core values and acceptable practices. With agreement about these big things, the smaller things like standards often fall in line. Principles can vary from one participant to the next—nonprofits espouse principles that may vary from for-profits, small private companies may possess values that vary in some respects from big public corporations, organizations based in countries such as China, India, or Russia may have norms that are culturally at odds with those in Western countries. Finding principles that everyone can live with, then, is essential. Agreeing to a set of principles helps set parameters around how people solve the problem facing the collaboration; it defines clearly what's acceptable and what's not, avoiding time-wasting and conflict-producing detours.

As governor of Utah, I was active in the Western Governors Association. All the member states experienced common pain, and the organization prided itself in taking a nonpartisan approach to working together. For example, Governor John Kitzhaber of Oregon and I often collaborated in developing environmental policies for the WGA. He is a Democrat, and I am a Republican. Despite our different political affiliations and perspectives, we shared many values. At a meeting in Alaska, the governors discussed common environmental issues we faced in a private meeting over lunch. We concluded that despite our shared values, we often didn't communicate with each other effectively because we hadn't devoted enough time to choosing words to express ourselves in ways that reflected our common beliefs.

Governor Kitzhaber and I agreed to work at framing a series of common principles for the governors to agree upon, regardless of political party. Over several months, we refined a list of principles that formed the basis of an environmental doctrine. We gave the doctrine a name, "En Libra," drawn from two Latin words that captured the overall theme of our agreement. *En* (move toward) and *Libra* (balance). Here is our list:

- Collaboration, not polarization
- Reward results, not programs
- Science for facts, process for priorities
- Markets before mandates
- Change a heart, change a nation

- Recognition of costs and benefits
- Solutions transcend national boundaries

The WGA members enthusiastically embraced the doctrine of En Libra. When we were working to develop a multistate policy on difficult subjects like the movement of nuclear waste across state lines or the enhancement of air quality, we would start with the principles of En Libra and create policies with great efficiency. Because the principles were in place, it took us much less time and talk to figure out our assumptions, standards, and sources.

Information Gathering and Dissemination

Information asymmetries are the bane of collaboration. Typically, they involve disconnects between the information base of one participant and that of another. While these asymmetries can have a variety of causes, the most common one is natural bias. People rely reflexively on certain information because it provides a basis for achieving outcomes beneficial to their organizations. As part of the effort to reform the health care system in New Orleans after Hurricane Katrina, we discussed building a new hospital as part of the solution to the problems that plagued the city. Some participants wanted to build this hospital, while others didn't. The pro-hospital forces projected high revenues from this future facility, while the anti-hospital group was working with projected revenues that were significantly lower.

To avoid asymmetries, collaborations must agree on the existing data (formal research, white papers, indexes, and so on) from which they'll work. In addition, they must agree to work together rather than separately on any fact-finding project. Third, they need to share information equally among all participants and do so regularly and on a timely basis. Typically, collaborators use various forms of technology (Dropbox, Google Docs, shared servers, or cloud storage systems, to name a handful in use as of this writing) to create a common information base.

WHY GREAT COLLABORATIONS RUN
ON THE SAME RAIL GAUGE

Before Congress, at the behest of President Lincoln, created a standard gauge (distance between the two rails) of 4 feet 8½ inches, railroads throughout the United States used seven different gauges.[3] The lack of a standard gauge meant that a train that ran on one kind of track couldn't run on another, and so railroad companies could not create any national system to transport goods and people across the country. This inefficient system greatly increased transportation costs. Only when the standard gauge was mandated by law in 1862 did the situation improve.

Without consensus on assumptions, standards, and sources and information, collaborations are in the same position as U.S. railroads before 1862. People can't maximize the productivity inherent in a collaboration without this consensus. Either they'll run along smoothly for a while until they encounter a different gauge, or they'll bicker constantly and often with increasing acrimony about which gauge is best. In either instance, the lack of uniformity creates problems.

Introducing these issues at the start of the collaboration may seem like asking for trouble. If you're the convener or leader, you may worry that grappling with potentially divisive subjects like principles or proprietary information at the beginning may force a wedge between participants. This is a possibility, but it's preferable to allowing these issues to surface down the road, after time, money, and energy have been invested. This is a test of participants' ability to work together. Are they willing to make the compromises that will allow them to collaborate effectively? Is the common pain sufficient that they'll accept what they regard as a less-than-ideal operational standard in order to alleviate the pain? Do all participants demonstrate a willingness and ability to engage in spirited discussions on these matters without letting the debate become personal and destructive?

Surescripts increased its odds of becoming a highly effective collaboration because its members established standards at the outset. Before this collaboration existed, the two segments of the industry—pharmacies and PBMs—used their own separate electronic systems to route pharmaceutical information. When they joined forces, they had to agree on a common system, which meant a great deal of compromising and negotiating about the standards.

The Constitutional Convention, too, relied on common standards and information. From the very beginning, participants agreed to tackle the issues they faced sequentially and formally. At the start, they agreed to work as a group to create a document rather than assign the work to a small, powerful committee.

In fact, in just about every collaboration we've led or participated in, we've found that the outcome is much better when people operate from an established common base of standards and information, rather than just assuming that they're doing so. When people wrongly assume they're on the same track—which is common—then this issue emerges only when the collaboration readies its recommendations or makes its final decision. It's at this point that a representative will say, "Oh! I thought we were working from Index A, and now it turns out that you actually were following that ridiculous Index B." Or: "Now that you're putting the so-called solution in writing, I can see that you have based it on the belief that we need to implement it nationally, while we were sure it was only going to be a properly cautious regional approach."

As an example of withholding information, organizations might refuse to disclose their original research or other knowledge that they believe is proprietary—either they don't mention that they have the information or they admit they have it but insist that revealing it would rob them of a well-earned competitive advantage (or give a competitor an advantage). While organizations can legitimately claim that certain knowledge is proprietary, there are better ways around this issue than withholding it or pretending it doesn't exist.

Perception is reality. If some participants believe others are using information to gain leverage over the collaboration or hiding critical data, it will create anger, frustration, and conflict down the line. Similarly, if the ground rules of process and procedures aren't detailed and if decisions aren't made on everything from language to measures of progress, then the uncertainty or ambiguity will work against the collaboration. Even when everyone is aboveboard and honest, the lack of established standards may cause members to perceive that they are being manipulated. At the very least, it may create doubt in some people's minds about how fair the process is—doubt that can simmer and build into distrust.

HOW TO FIND AND ESTABLISH COMMON GROUND

In some instances, establishing commonalities is relatively easy. When the common pain is bad enough and at least some of the other elements of a value alliance are in place (a convener of stature, representatives of substance), then establishing basic operating procedures and information protocols comes naturally. People are willing to compromise and agree on standards because they recognize intuitively that it's necessary.

In other instances, however, the problem may not be big enough to motivate participants to accept a scientific basis for moving forward or to agree to language that strikes them as off target. This level of disagreement is more likely in collaborations where participants are antagonistic competitors or where global and cultural diversity make it challenging to establish common standards.

To create common standards and information processes from the beginning, even in the face of early tension and challenges, we've had good results with these tactics:

- Create transparency.
- Find a third party to interpret and communicate information.
- Anticipate disagreements.
- Impose certain standards in certain situations.
- Adopt and adapt information principles.

Create Transparency

When leaders and conveners don't establish a rule that information is accessible to all representatives and provide a method to access it, then transparency doesn't happen—and real collaboration is unlikely. Creating transparency starts with conveners and leaders, but they need to formalize this concept rather than simply verbalizing it. From the beginning, the charter should state that all information arising from the collaboration's efforts—reports, research, project notes, decisions—is available to every participant. Similarly, the technology should be set up to facilitate access to this information.

The Streamlined Sales Tax Governing Board collaboration engaged diverse representatives (from eighteen different states) and faced a complex mass of legal and financial issues, so establishing a methodology to exchange information and update members on new developments was crucial. For this reason, the board created a website that made available a huge amount of information, from formal papers to meeting topics to decisions made. In this way, it created the transparency necessary to assure all representatives that everyone was operating from the same information base.[4]

Find a Third Party

Transparency will not be achieved when side projects or secret research studies are known only to a select group of participants. It is highly desirable to reach consensus on what organizations are obligated to share with members—and on how to deal with information that won't be shared.

Conflict sometimes arises because participants are unwilling to share white papers, research studies, focus group findings, surveys, and other data that they've created on their own. Protecting proprietary data can be a big problem when competitors are collaborating, and it can lead to dissension when information that seems relevant to the aim of the collaboration is withheld.

Many times, the problem is that a given organization fears that revealing proprietary information will give competitors an edge—or rob it of its own edge. Hiring a third party—an outside consultant or respected figure in the field—can provide a solution. This third party can scrub the data and make sure that the collaboration still benefits from the work done by a member without revealing key aspects of that data that might hurt the company that did the original work.

For instance, a health care collaboration consisted of a number of highly competitive hospitals, and a few of the hospitals were reluctant to reveal what the outcomes were for certain types of procedures—they didn't want their competitors to know their success rates in these areas. They worried about the impact of this information on comparative advertising campaigns, Internet news, or stories in traditional media. At the same time, this data was essential to help ease the common pain all participants were facing (a rising rate of hospital-acquired infections, among other problems). They hired a health care industry consultant to assess the data and provide cumulative results of the analysis without revealing which outcomes came from which hospitals.

Anticipate Disagreements

Many committed leaders and conveners can assess their representatives and recognize where the tension points will be. They know that the CEO of Company A is extremely sensitive when it comes to the issue of using low-cost labor from third-world countries; they know that the head of a government agency is adamant about curbing labor abuses in these countries. Consequently, the two individuals are likely to disagree when it comes to establishing metrics for their collaboration's work on fair labor practices around the world. Conveners and committed leaders, anticipating this disagreement, can open a discussion about this issue early on and see if they can find a compromise metric that satisfies both parties.

Before work begins, create a list of who is most likely to disagree and a list of what they're likely to disagree about. In terms of the who, figure out who has clashed in the past: competitors with each other, business and regulatory agencies, business and consumer activist groups, and so on. You might also observe interactions between representatives at the initial collaborative meeting, noting who rubs whom the wrong way because of opposing personal styles or belligerent attitudes.

In terms of the what, identify the hot button issues that surround possible solutions to the common pain. Your group probably has a number of options in terms of formulating solutions. The problem might be addressed locally, regionally, nationally, or globally. The solution might involve spending $1 million, $10 million, or $20 million. The group might rely on a study that predicts the problem will reach crisis proportions before the end of the year—or on another study that suggests it won't research a crisis stage for at least another ten years. By identifying these options and what representatives might disagree about, you can get the disagreements out in the open and use dialogue to either find common ground or at least start a conversation that might lead to compromise.

Another, more positive way to defuse potential disagreements is to create an inventory of matters the collaboration must agree upon. Use the five categories listed earlier—existing facts and figures, operating procedures, language, principles, and information gathering and dissemination—as a base for this inventory, tailoring it to the specific issues your collaboration is facing.

Impose Certain Standards In Certain Situations

Ideally, participants will work through their disagreements relatively quickly and reach consensus on the standards and information assumptions that govern the collaboration. If arguments persist, however, and it seems as if the lack of agreement is endangering the collaboration's mission, then the convener can impose standards on the group—if the conditions are right. Essentially, *the right conditions* means that the convener possesses a significant amount of power. The most obvious example: The convener is the president of the United States. Or: The convener is the CEO of one of the world's largest corporations. Or: The convener is a highly influential figure in the sector where many representatives work—Chicago's former Mayor Richard Daley in politics, Bill Gates in the software world, Nelson Mandela in the global arena.

Imposing standards is not without risk. No one, especially not representatives of substance who are powerful in their own right, likes to be told what standards or information protocols they must adhere to. A representative who strongly disagrees with what is being imposed may walk away from the collaboration. Generally, however, the combination of a powerful convener and a high level of common pain will be sufficient to keep representatives at the table, no matter how much they might disagree with the imposed standard.

Adopt and Adapt Information Principles

When a collaboration needs to do original research or when information relating to science and technology is involved, it helps to agree on some general principles before any of the actual work is done. At the EPA, for example, we adopted these four principles to help environmental collaborations share information readily and openly:

- Engage in joint fact-finding.
- Align science with policy deliberation.
- Provide capacity where appropriate.
- Share information widely.

The joint fact-finding effort helped ensure that all collaborators shared a common information base. We expected participants to work jointly to identify key questions, assemble the relevant information, and determine how to address information gaps.

Aligning science with policy deliberation meant that scientific analysis would inform deliberations about policy issues. At the same time, policy dialogue would structure scientific inquiry to keep it useful and relevant to the problem at hand.

To ensure that all stakeholders were sufficiently knowledgeable and able to understand necessary information, the EPA agreed to provide stakeholders with the capacity to obtain independent technical assistance where necessary. Meanwhile, it was agreed that broad dissemination of information regarding both process and substance would enhance the transparency of collaborative processes. The principles emphasized that particular attention should be given to ensure that populations at risk and other marginalized groups had access to information.

At the EPA, we found that these four principles did a lot to help ensure that participants feel included and equal. Feel free to adopt them as is, or to adapt them to the information requirements of your collaboration.

CAN YOU AGREE?

Defining common standards boils down to the capacity of collaborators to reach foundational agreements. At the start of the process, participants may have different ideas about solutions to the problem that confronts them—which is fine, since it takes a good deal of discussion, research, and creativity to hit upon a recommendation or decision that everyone buys into. But to get to the point—and to hold the collaboration together until that point is reached—agreement about operating modes and information protocols is necessary.

We've been part of collaborations where participants arrived with very different perspectives on information sharing, vocabulary, and ways of getting things done, yet they were able to overcome these differences and find common ground. Shortly after the 9/11 attacks, for example, we were part of a collaboration designed to respond to anthrax-based terrorism. The partners in this collaboration were a wide variety of federal agencies, each of which had its own information protocols, acronyms, and modes of operation. All the participants had to agree to share information with each other and to define what constituted an anthrax event requiring a response. Somewhat surprisingly, participants achieved consensus on these and other issues quickly, and during the 2002 Winter Olympics in Utah, when a false positive was triggered at the airport, the collaboration responded to the alarm flawlessly.

Agreement on standards and information at the outset of a collaboration can be a significant challenge. It can be somewhat shocking when diverse participants come together and it turns out that participating organizations harbor dramatically different ideas on measures, behaviors, and methods. In our negotiations on food and drug safety issues with China, we came to realize that underlying cultural differences had a significant impact in the early negotiations. The Chinese argued that U.S. concerns regarding melamine tainted pet food and lead paint on toys were more a product of our press than of real safety concerns. We came to understand our differences relative to the press and it was a helpful reminder that we had adopted different scientific standards, methodologies, and safety practices, all of which had to be incorporated into our attempts to ensure product safety for U.S. consumers. From the most basic differences in our government processes to our divergent views of the role and nature of the media, we started with significant cultural distinctions. Over time we began to understand and recognize that our objective was to improve safety outcomes, standards, and measures in ways that would create interoperability between our systems.

And you don't have to be dealing with another country or culture to encounter different standards and information perspectives—the company down the block or in the next state may start from expectations completely different from your own. That's why collaborations must bring common standards into the open early, discuss them thoroughly, and determine if agreement is possible. If not, then the collaboration is probably doomed no matter what other elements are in place. If these issues are addressed and resolved, however, the collaborative partners have added an element that is essential for the creation of a value alliance.

TEN

Collaborative Intelligence

Not everyone has a natural aptitude or appetite for collaborative problem solving. Though effective collaboration requires a skill that can be learned and improved, some people are naturally better at collaboration than others.

I learned this after finishing a major collaborative project, when I asked a former judge to capture the history and lessons learned from the project to assist others in similar ventures in the future. The judge demurred, saying he found collaborative writing projects frustrating and preferred to work on them when he had complete control. His candor was rare for two reasons. First, most people aren't sufficiently aware of their own collaborative capacity. Second, even if they are aware, they tend not to admit it to others—either concealing their reluctance when they agree or citing other factors when they decline assignments requiring this skill.

Alliance success is threatened when the wrong people—the ones lacking what we refer to as *collaborative intelligence* (CI)—participate. CI, the ability to work productively together for a common goal, is a critical ingredient for successful value alliances. While we've addressed the need for this ability in our discussion of the eight elements, it is still useful to develop a deeper understanding of what CI is and how it helps build high-functioning alliances. This type of intelligence helps a group acquire and manage all the value alliance elements. If an alliance possesses a sufficiently high level of CI, it can overcome participants' natural resistance to ceding control to an independent entity, and it can facilitate productive interactions among diverse individuals and organizations.

CI is more than being friendly or having a cooperative attitude. While there's nothing wrong with these traits, we've also worked with irascible, dogmatic, sarcastic people who had high levels of CI. In any given network or alliance, you'll find a wide range of personalities, and you cannot identify collaborative intelligence by whether someone is loud or quiet, gregarious or reticent. Intelligence is not predictor of CI, nor is charisma.

On top of that, it's not just the capacity of one individual that matters but the collective CI of the group. Invariably, a diverse group will possess representatives with varying degrees of CI. As wonderful as it would be to have all representatives possessing equally high collaborative abilities, it probably won't happen. Therefore, your assessment of CI needs to focus on the whole rather than the parts. You need to look at the collective CI of the group and determine if it's sufficient to solve the complex problem the group has been convened to address.

This factor is key to determining if you should become involved in building or joining an alliance. Increasingly, the world is organizing itself into collaborative networks as a means of achieving competitiveness. In the future, success will be defined by the collaborative alliances you form or join. Participation in an alliance is an investment decision because it allocates your resources, including time, money, and people. Not every alliance is worth your time and effort, so you need to be astute in your assessment.

While you can and should attempt to determine the CI of prospective representatives prior to the start of the collaboration, you probably won't be able to judge the CI of many participants until you've worked with them over a matter of weeks or months. Keep in mind that CI directly impacts the sociology of the collaboration—the higher the level of CI in your group, the more likely it is to function as a value alliance. When a collaboration possesses a great deal of collaborative intelligence, its members are able to overcome formidable obstacles and solve even the most complex of problems.

FIVE CRUCIAL TRAITS OF CI

Collaborative intelligence may sound like a scientific term, but we're not psychologists or researchers. Instead, our definition of CI is purely empirical, resulting from having built, led, or participated in hundreds of alliances. We have observed the following five critical traits in gifted collaborators.

Empathetic

High-CI people are secure enough to embrace the advice given by Stephen R. Covey, the author of *Seven Habits of Highly Effective People:* "Seek first to understand, then to be understood."[1] People with high collaborative intelligence make an effort to understand the views and needs of others; they listen honestly, thoughtfully, and objectively. They don't lock into positions prematurely. While they may possess strong points of view, they make an effort to hear other perspectives and will adjust their points of view once convinced they need adjusting.

No doubt, you've worked with people who possess this trait. They are a pleasure to work with because they are driven to work productively with others to achieve the goals of the group. They willingly share ideas and information, communicate straightforwardly, and engage with anyone who can help achieve the common objective.

This trait played a major role in the story of Surescripts (told in Chapter One). The owners of the two rival organizations had and continue to have substantially different economic and policy interests that create a natural competitive tension. On top of that, they are both strong-minded, intellectually keen, and immensely competitive. Yet they both manage to listen to each other with seriousness and understanding, and this ability goes a long way toward sustaining their highly successful alliance.

Listening is also a by-product of consensus decision-making. Because everyone's opinion has value, listening becomes a more valued competency. Eventually, advocacy and positional bargaining become less important than listening to everyone's point of view and weighing the relative value of every position expressed. Listening for this deeper understanding is a fundamental component of effective collaborations.

Optimistic, with an Abundance Mentality

Optimism is a more subtle trait than empathy but no less important. If you're like most people, you've worked with individuals who treated every interaction as if it were a competition. Seeing every situation as win-lose, they are reluctant to concede a point or offer assistance. They turn calm discussions into fierce debates, pout when a point doesn't go in their favor, and gloat when it does.

An optimistic abundance mentality, on the other hand, means seeing beyond immediate needs and desires to the long-term ideal. These people view the world in terms of plenty rather than scarcity. For them, the effort of a group can result in win-win situations—they can benefit and so can competitors. Part and parcel of this abundance mentality is one of opportunity. Even problems are viewed through the lens of opportunity, in that solutions offer the chance to do things more quickly, more efficiently, and more productively.

In our preparation for the 2002 Utah Winter Olympic Games, we faced a significant challenge because emergency responders and law enforcement agencies were using incompatible communication systems. The national government had recently freed part of the radio communications spectrum for use by emergency responders and made it mandatory that every agency adopt this new frequency range by a specific date. Regrettably, little coordination existed among agencies making this transition, a lot of money had to be spent to make it happen, and some incompatibility between systems would remain.

To solve this problem, I found allies among all state and local police and emergency response units in Utah. The biggest challenge was that the local police and fire departments wanted to control their own systems. I asked the chiefs of police and fire departments to come to the governor's mansion, where I proposed a collaborative development of a common solution.

Many law enforcement officers are command-and-control leaders; their culture teaches them to act decisively and authoritatively, and they are not particularly good at cooperating with outside agencies. Fortunately, as part of the convening process, we had identified a group of participants with an abundance mentality. They were individuals who recognized that working together would produce a result far superior to what they could get on their own. As a result, these law enforcement leaders spoke affirmatively at the meeting and asserted their commitment to solving the problem. By the end of the meeting, while some still didn't like the idea of sharing control of the emergency communication system, the whole group was working together toward what would become the Utah Communication Agency Network (UCAN), the backbone of emergency communication statewide.

Principle-Focused

In *Getting to Yes*, Roger Fisher, Bruce Patton, and William Ury discuss the concepts of principle-based negotiation and position-based negotiation.[2] In the former, people discuss and debate according to principle rather than exclusively on the basis of their self-interest. Principle-based negotiators focus on the issues to be resolved (rather than on people, which can lead to personality conflicts and arguing for argument's sake). Those who negotiate from a position-based perspective can take an extreme stance, dig in, and refuse to listen to other opinions or to accept alternative views—losing the opportunity to create a solution that may, in fact, be better for all parties involved.

It's great when people make their ideals or beliefs known and campaign for solutions to problems dovetailing with these principles. When they argue or disagree, it's based on bedrock values. They keep discussions on this higher level and don't get personal, making them good collaborators.

In the American West, few matters evoke stronger emotions than the management of publicly owned land. National advocacy groups push for large tracts of land to be preserved as wilderness, where access is restricted and nearly all economic use is prohibited. Others, often local people, want the land to be used in ways that generate an economic future for their community. In the West, several states have most of their land mass under the control and management of the federal government. This was true in Utah—the federal government owns nearly 75 percent of all land there, which was a source of constant and often bitter conflict when I was governor.

Some of this federal land, however, was given in trust for the state's school children. This school land is spread all over the state, and some of it is in environmentally sensitive areas. As a result, when we tried to develop some of the land for our schools, the federal government or advocacy groups got nervous about the environmental impacts and blocked our efforts, creating litigation and political nightmares.

This problem existed for a hundred years, and though governors of various Western states tried to solve the problem, they made little progress. When I was governor, though, I approached Secretary of Interior Bruce Babbitt, the former governor of Arizona, and suggested we identify pieces of school trust land inside national parks, monuments, or other sensitive areas the federal government felt it necessary to control, and that we trade that land for blocks of federal land of equal value in areas where development would not pose a problem. That would allow the state to develop them on behalf of its schoolchildren and eliminate some of the painful conflict between the state and the federal government. He liked the idea. Secretary Babbit and I agreed that we would use our joint stature to convene a process that could collaboratively put together a proposal.

However, before forming the team to develop the proposal, we decided to hammer out a set of principles to guide our effort. Here are the principles included in the charter:

- Approximate Equal Value
- Ignore the Critics
- Sharing Data

- Leadership and Role Clarification
- Confidentiality
- Working with Key Stakeholders

Each of these principles was developed enough to let others be sure of what we meant. The first, for example, made it clear that the goal was to create a fair deal—knowing it would be impossible to be precise about values. We wanted a deal that would preserve these key inholdings and fairly compensate the state, and would have good conservation and good economic benefits. We agreed these goals were equal and we must always characterize the deal as being fair and of approximately equal value.

After several months of work, a collaborative proposal was produced. Utah received 139,000 acres of federal land and $50 million in cash in exchange for all the school trust land located inside national parks, monuments, forests, and other federal areas. It was the largest U.S. land exchange since the Louisiana Purchase. Without the principles agreed to by Secretary Babbitt and me, and ratified by the participants, this complex land-use tangle would still be plaguing the state and federal governments.

Transparent

Transparency is essential to a successful alliance because trust is at the heart of alliance building. Without trust, collaboration becomes negotiation, not a problem-solving exercise. Transparency means being willing to share not only information but your own genuine feelings and perspectives, even if you know that they make you vulnerable to criticism. When people reveal little of their thoughts and feelings, it engenders suspicion. Transparency, however, clears the air. Even though some collaborative partners might not like your viewpoint, they'll respect your honesty in sharing it consistently.

Outcome-Oriented

High-CI people pursue overall team outcomes instead of individual win-lose statistics. This attitude facilitates collaboration because it helps the group pull together toward a common objective—people do their jobs to the best of their ability rather than getting sidetracked on creating impressive-sounding reports, generating favorable publicity, or seeking other ways to deliver good scorecards. While effective conveners, leaders, and representatives all tend to be highly influential people with healthy egos, they are able to subordinate their own desire for personal fame or gain to the positive outcome the alliance is targeting.

General Stanley McChrystal demonstrated all five of these collaborative intelligence traits when he led the Joint Special Operations Command from 2003 to 2008 and served as commander of U.S. and NATO forces in Afghanistan in 2009 and 2010. Despite the U.S. military's superior weaponry and size, it was struggling to defeat the Taliban when General McChrystal was appointed as U.S. and NATO commander. The problem was that the Taliban operated as a network—its units were extremely mobile, fast, and flexible. They were often able to hit and move on before we could react.

General McChrystal recognized that to be effective against al Qaeda and the Taliban, U.S. forces needed to operate more as a network and less as a gigantic, poorly coordinated command-and-control structure. As a four-star general with tremendous position power, he could have ordered all the various entities under his command—Navy, Army, Marines, Air Force, Coast Guard, CIA, and so on—to work together differently. While his orders would have been obeyed, they would have been obeyed without enthusiasm or deep commitment.

For this reason, General McChrystal used questions, one-on-one conversations, and influence to move his forces to a more networked style of operating. He was transparent with his people about why he was suggesting that drone videos be shared with all relevant parties rather than selectively parceled out: it wasn't about gaining glory for one part of the military but about how all participating entities would gain if they could establish an effective network (an abundance mentality). He also used his great interpersonal skills to foster a cooperative mindset among all the diverse groups under his command, going so far as to house them all in one tent instead of letting them operate in their customary separate locations. As a result, General McChrystal's Joint Operations Command cohered as a network and greatly increased its combat effectiveness.[3]

For contrast, it's useful look at someone with low CI and see how this affects the operation of a group. In 2009, we were asked to work with the representatives of four large, highly competitive corporations on a safety issue that plagued their industry. They asked us to help them identify how they might work together to solve the problem, and our meeting came up with fifteen possible approaches. Three of the representatives demonstrated high CI and engaged in great discussions about these possibilities. The fourth representative—speaking, unfortunately, for the largest of the companies—sabotaged the discussions. No matter what anyone suggested, the response was always a variation on "That won't work" or "We're already working on that," and no new suggestions were forthcoming. Instead, every remark revealed a primary concern with achieving a private agenda—not in addressing the larger problem the group was trying to solve. The saboteur was opaque rather than transparent, bristling at suggestions that it would be useful to reveal some proprietary research into this safety issue, and both deaf to a principle-focus and wholly lacking an abundance mentality—clearly convinced that it would be much more advantageous to solve the safety issue independently (and reap all the favorable publicity) than to do so as part of a larger group.

As a result, the life drained out of the group whenever this representative spoke, and without the largest company in their industry the other three representatives were unable to save the collaboration.

You want to be able to spot the saboteurs as soon as possible, and this chapter will provide the tools for doing so. First, though, it's useful to understand how CI can turn self-interested negotiators into mutually interested collaborators.

DIVERSE COUNTRIES, CULTURES, CONCERNS

In 2007, Rich received a call from Andy von Eschenbach, commissioner of the Food and Drug Administration (FDA), informing him that various pet food products imported into the United States from China were contaminated with melamine. We were importing an increasingly large number of products from China and safety issues were a growing concern not only in this country but in China. As secretary of HHS, I appointed Rich to head a collaborative group with representatives from the United States and China to negotiate new and improved safety standards for imports.

As you might imagine, many potential points of conflict existed. In the United States, there was tremendous concern about the safety of imports from China and suspicion that Chinese standards were far below those mandated by the FDA. For China, the melamine problem represented the kind of serious financial loss that occurs when imported products are denied entry. Even worse, perhaps, was the damage done to the Chinese brand—people were wary of buying products with "made in China" labels.

Had the members of our collaborative group lacked collaborative intelligence, the process would have been a disaster. There were plenty of opportunities for accusations and cross-accusations: "Your country [the United States] is overreacting to the problem because of your distrust of our country." And: "Your country [China] lacks the high safety standards that we insist upon in the United States." The process could have turned into a destructive negotiation where neither side considered the other's position and issues.

Fortunately, these acrimonious exchanges didn't take place among our collaborators. At the commencement of our discussions and prior to the actual negotiations, the Chinese sent two important government officials I had worked with in the past: Minister Gao of the Ministry of Health and Minister Li of the General Administration of Quality Supervision and Inspection and Quarantine. Additional U.S. representatives included FDA and HHS officials as well as those from other government agencies and private corporations that did business with China.

The common pain was intense, in large part because the media had gotten hold of the story in this country and created alarm if not outright panic. Thus all participants were motivated to ease this pain. But without a high level of CI, they would have failed to do so. In any collaboration of diverse cultures and perspectives, conflicts can occur, and this one was no different.

What was truly amazing about our conversations was the degree of transparency. Both the U.S. representatives and the Chinese were open and honest throughout the process. Each of us talked about the limitations of our respective systems and about what we hoped to accomplish in the future. Rich, too, was crucial in keeping the focus on solving the problem so that there was a mutually beneficial outcome. Rich, who has a high level of CI, used qualities such as an abundance mentality and a principles-focus as well as transparency to keep the collaboration at a high level.

These CI traits paid off. We established a set of agreements that improved safety standards not only for food but for drugs and devices as well. When other safety problems emerged after these discussions, the agreements were enormously useful in helping both countries respond to the problems quickly and effectively.

TOGETHERNESS WHEN THINGS GET TOUGH

Because collaborations are relatively fragile entities—not held together by an act of incorporation or long-standing history and culture—they require individuals who possess strong interpersonal skills and positive, inclusive attitudes (that is, the five traits of CI). It doesn't take much to create a rift in a collaboration, one that can widen and destroy it. Here are two reasons that collaborative groups may shatter like fragile glass when bumped:

- *Constant arguing and in-fighting.* Acrimonious debate that occurs regularly and appears irresolvable can discourage everyone and can reduce morale so far that the group falls apart.
- *Sustained inaction.* Inactivity can be as bad as acrimony. For any number of reasons—including the fact that no one has a CEO's positional authority to dictate decisions—the coalition can't implement anything. The dithering drives everyone away.

To maintain the collaboration through arguments and inaction, representatives must have high CI. If they do, they can keep debates civil; they can also keep the discussion going during lulls and talk honestly and openly about why nothing is happening and what might be done about it. In some complex negotiations with foreign governments, a committee works to negotiate an agreement with these governments and then brings the final document to all the relevant parties at the last hour. While this may be efficient, it is also insensitive; it can create anger and resentment because these parties are treated as afterthoughts.

In the melamine example, Rich regularly briefed and included all the groups of interested parties, both government and private sector, at each stage of the process, ensuring a sense of participation and gaining buy-in. This made sure that everyone was on board and no one would throw a wrench into the works at the last minute.

Similarly, the main representative for the Chinese government, Minister Li, possessed a great deal of CI. Principle-focused and cooperative without being quiescent, Minister Li sat with both of us in one particularly tense negotiation session. Had a minister with lower CI been involved, he might well have ended the negotiations then and there. Minister Li, however, kept the conversation civil and focused on the ultimate goal, and though this was preliminary to the negotiations, it set the stage for a continually productive relationship. He sought us out shortly thereafter and said, "The problems we had today, we understand your point and we think you're right, we do have a problem. We think we can work with you."

More than anything else, this conciliatory gesture helped posture the negotiations for a win-win solution to the problem.

WHAT DOES COLLECTIVE COLLABORATIVE INTELLIGENCE LOOK LIKE?

People's personalities in collaborations are as diverse as their backgrounds, organizations, and perspectives. Individuals who possess high CI are not necessarily agreeable, empathetic, and polite. Therefore, the collaborative process is not always a smooth one. Vociferous debates, raised voices, and temporary deadlocks may occur even among people who work well together.

While animation pioneer Pixar Studios may be more a corporate entity than a diverse network of organizations, it epitomizes a highly successful collaborative collective. Ed Catmull, who was chief technology officer of Pixar and now is the president of Walt Disney Animation Studios, talked to us in 2000 about the collaborative culture that permeates Pixar. The internal Pixar University teaches collaborative skills to animators and programmers, and this formal emphasis on working productively together encourages employees to develop and use their natural collaborative abilities to amplify one another's work. At Pixar, daily collaborative reviews are conducted to allow teams to examine their work in progress without embarrassment—the reviews are supportively constructive rather than demeaning or demanding. Teamwork is emphasized while lone-wolf pursuit of achievement is not.

In environments where high CI exists, people react differently to common work situations than the norm. For instance, when low-CI work groups face a crisis, failure, or serious problem, people tend to react with cynicism, negativity, and blaming. In a high-CI group, on the other hand, the typical reaction is increased productivity. This group understands that the solution to the problem resides in applying their collective knowledge and skills to help each other work toward a solution, and that means that problems or setbacks catalyze a greater output of energy and effort. Individuals in a high-CI group may still be angry with each other (and privately believe that Joe or Mary or someone else was responsible for the current problem), but they vent through productivity rather than scapegoating or other uncollaborative behaviors.

Another characteristic of collectively high CI is that people share ideas and information all along the way, not just at the end. Doing so helps the group work more productively and with less friction. When teams are continuously apprised of changes or have access to a flow of ideas and resources, they can adjust their strategies as they go along. In low-CI settings, people drop bombshells at the end of the process—they admit that the estimate for completion has changed or they reveal some other major piece of news that not only hampers the group's productivity but creates dissension—people are understandably resentful that someone waited until the last minute to provide a piece of crucial information.

Low-CI people hoard information for a number of reasons. If they're in a group with competitors, they fear what their competitors will do with the information they share. They may also selfishly keep a great idea under wraps until the end, wanting to play the role of hero and solve the problem when every other approach has failed. Whatever the reason, information hoarding often prevents the group from functioning effectively.

An effective collaborative group works smoothly in the face of tension between self-interest and the interest of the group. As noted earlier, people join value alliances out of self-interest—they're facing a problem that they would prefer to solve on their own but recognize they can get a better solution faster as part of a collaboration. Thus they need to prioritize the common interest over self-interest, and high-CI people can accommodate this gracefully. If you examine the airline industry, you will see this paradox everywhere you look. Airports are built and shared by competitors; so too are ground crews and reservation services. This didn't happen simultaneously but evolved as the airlines recognized collaboration helped all of them do their jobs more efficiently and profitably. Airlines still look out for their own self-interests, but they have found ways to compete on a collaborative foundation.

Therefore, don't assume that when you see a gathering of high-CI individuals you're viewing an altruistic, self-sacrificing group. What's distinctive is that they are sufficiently solution-oriented that they overcome their reluctance to share information, ideas, and resources with outsiders. They reach across the aisle and initiate discussions, volunteer assistance, and listen receptively.

If you've ever been on jury duty, you've witnessed the dynamic of collaboration in action, and if you're fortunate, you've served on a jury with high-CI people. In many ways, juries mirror value alliances. People from different walks of life are thrown together to deliver a just verdict—a verdict that (theoretically, at least) will be better reasoned than if a single person arrived at it. The twelve jury members need to learn to work together, and just as personality conflicts emerge quickly, so do individuals who are excellent communicators and enlighteners. High-CI juries debate, ask questions, share honest feelings, and focus on the outcome. Eventually, they arrive at a consensus verdict—one that feels fair to everyone even though some may have had questions and concerns along the way. Low-CI juries, on the other hand, either become hopelessly deadlocked or deliver a verdict that is the product of a few forceful individuals rather than true collaboration and consensus.

RESPONDING TO THE LOW-CI INDIVIDUAL

What happens if you're recruited to join a collaboration in which at least one person is obstreperous, selfish, and pursuing a private agenda rather than the group objective? What if you're the committed leader and you discover that one of your representatives is acting in ways that are preventing the group from making progress toward its goals?

The simplest course of action is to avoid getting into that sort of situation, or to withdraw from it as soon as you recognize it. That is, if you are invited into a collaboration where a number of individuals seem to be poor collaborators, then you should decline participation. You may feel honored that you've been asked to take part, and you may believe the group's purpose is worthy and other members are prestigious and influential people. But if you see a core of low-CI members, then it will be impossible to accomplish much, and you'll be frustrated at every turn and fail to solve the problem that the collaboration was set up to solve.

Bear in mind that it's easier to select people who are good collaborators than to train bad ones to acquire this competency. Collaborative skills can be developed and polished when people have some aptitude in this area; when they lack this aptitude, though, no amount of encouragement or training will help. When individuals are in the middle of the continuum—if they possess some collaborative skills but also have certain anticollaborative traits—then it's possible that they might move toward the right side of the continuum and become valuable contributors. It may take a committed leader sitting down with them and emphasizing the importance of exhibiting collaborative behaviors or it might help if someone else with influence uses that influence to convince them to behave themselves. It's unrealistic, however, to expect people who are low on the CI scale to transform into great collaborators just because they have joined a collaboration.

If you're the convener, it's your responsibility to search for representatives of substance and especially a committed leader with high collaborative intelligence. While it probably won't be possible to recruit uniformly high-CI representatives, you need to select with the collective CI in mind. Out of necessity, you may need to choose certain representatives with low CI because they possess the expertise, resources, or prestige the collaboration requires. However, you can attempt to raise the group CI by focusing on finding other representatives with high CI.

As the story of the failed safety collaboration demonstrates, a major player with poor CI can sabotage the entire group. On the other hand, value alliances can form and thrive despite the presence of a low-CI representative, as long as the individual doesn't command resources or information crucial to the group's success. A relatively minor player can be marginalized or even asked to leave the collaboration.

The consulting firm Talent+ refers to saboteurs as "onboard terrorists," and that term is appropriately alarming. By definition, saboteurs have low collaborative intelligence and in fact lower the group's collective CI by fomenting personality conflicts, taking the collaboration off on tangents, and doing other things that create dissension within the group. As difficult as it may be to do, the leader must negate the saboteur's influence, either through adroit maneuvering (assigning secondary tasks that preclude participation in core meetings) or by convincing the saboteur to leave.

IDENTIFYING CI LEVELS

As we've said, being friendly, easy-going, or a good listener doesn't necessarily mean someone has high CI. Because CI doesn't correspond to personality type, it's difficult to draw a definitive profile of a highly collaborative person. Both overbearing egotists and reflective altruists can have high CI, but we've crafted some guidelines to help give a sense of whether a given individual is high or low CI. The list of five identifying traits outlined earlier in this chapter—attentive, optimistic, principle-focused, transparent, and outcome-oriented—can act as a screen for choosing representatives of substance. Determining whether an individual actually has those traits can be a bit tricky, however, especially in a crisis or charged moment. Here are some tips for making a positive identification:

• *Rely on instinct combined with informed opinions.* If you've met and worked with prospective candidates for a collaboration, you already have a sense of how they might function in this new setting. You know if they were open or secretive about their feelings; whether they tried to bully you into their way of thinking or were open-minded. While your instinct won't always be right—they may have been on their best behavior when you met them (or, conversely, the situation may have made them act offensively)—it provides good guidance when combined with what others say. The kiss of death, collaboratively speaking, is when someone says, "John is difficult." *Difficult* may mean many things, but none of them are apt to be good from a collaborative perspective. If, on the other hand, people say, "John is *flexible* or *principled,*" then it may confirm your impression that this person will work productively with others. Ask yourself the following questions:

• Do they have good chemistry with other people?
• Do they avoid overreacting?
• Are they able to disagree in agreeable ways?
• Is their language respectful (rather than harsh or accusatory)?
• Do they possess a clear picture of goals without being stuck on only one path to reach them?
• Are they patient?
• Are the interests of the group in conflict with their own agendas?
• Are they more inclined to share than to keep things to and for themselves?
• Are they more positive than negative in outlook?

People who like working in silos, who are driven by personal agendas, and who enjoy manipulating others tend to have low CI. On the other hand, people who operate from a sense of principle tend to have high CI. Principle helps you see past the short-term obstacles and strive for ambitious, articulated objectives with great integrity. These qualities help people collaborate reasonably, productively, and most of all, intelligently.

ELEVEN

Alliance Enterprises
When and How to Create Ongoing Collaborations

Value alliances are created to solve problems, so logic suggests that when a problem is solved, the need for the value alliance is gone. This has been the case for many of the alliances described here, including the Constitutional Convention and the post-Katrina health care reform effort in New Orleans. In some instances, the value alliance dissolves even when the problem isn't completely solved but the common pain has eased sufficiently. In other instances, it ends when the problem has changed in scope and type and requires a new value alliance. And in still other situations, the collaboration closes up shop because the problem has proved too intractable for participants to resolve.

Some value alliances, however, put down roots. Western Governors University, Surescripts, GEOSS, and many others became established organizations with ongoing businesses and permanent governance models. Some were originally seen by their conveners as possessing a limited purpose and life span, but circumstances demonstrated a continuing need for their existence and they were turned into permanent enterprises. In other situations, however, conveners recognized from the start that the problems addressed by the alliance were ongoing and would require a continuous solution.

We call these long-term arrangements *alliance enterprises*. While they've existed in various forms for years, they are becoming increasingly common and increasingly effective in a range of industries and endeavors. In many ways, they represent a parallel competitive universe. People or organizations band together to ease the common pain, then recognize that the new network is better than any of them at solving a range of present and emerging problems.

Lloyd's of London is one of the earliest examples. It acts as an insurance company now, but it wasn't created as an ongoing organization. At its inception, ship captains met at Lloyd's Coffee House in London to exchange promises to share losses at sea prior to a voyage; they brought together allies and formed an alliance. When the voyage ended, the alliance no longer existed. However, ship owners concluded that their captains had identified an ongoing need, and that having a permanent organization would provide stability and value. Based on that conclusion, they formed Lloyd's of London as a business entity with a formal structure and rules of operation. The same collaborative functions took place when Lloyd's was a temporary entity, but its processes were facilitated by the alliance enterprise framework. To understand how this permanent organization facilitates collaborative processes, it's useful to consider how alliance enterprises differ from temporary value alliances.

THREE KEY TRAITS

Three characteristics differentiate permanent alliances from temporary ones:

- Legal status
- Business model
- Self-perpetuating corporate governance

These characteristics don't necessarily make alliance enterprises better than value alliances, but they do make them better suited to certain groups in certain situations.

Legal Status

Most value alliances start as unincorporated associations. They may have formalized their work through the creation of a charter, but generally the staffing is provided by one of the member organizations, or a consultant. They frequently borrow (from a participant's organization, for instance) or rent accommodations. Their mission is a temporary one and financial requirements are met by a fiscal agent who gathers funds either as voluntary contributions from a participant or participants or by way of an assessment.

Alliance enterprises, because of their permanent nature, generally need their own employees, the capacity to contract independently, the ability to accumulate assets, and other features of any ongoing organization. They have these requirements because they want to achieve a defined and independent legal status. While some achieve permanence as unincorporated associations, a corporation is usually formed to provide the legal capacity necessary to establish a business presence. Alliance enterprises are generally nonprofit organizations, but organizers may contribute capital with the goal of creating a self-sustaining enterprise that eventually attracts other participants, generating permanent value that can be monetized later.

Business Model

Alliance enterprises have a defined revenue model. In non-enterprise alliances, financial needs are generally met through member assessments of cash and matching contributions. In alliance enterprises, participants take on the characteristics of customers and the management of the alliance must develop a value proposition to hold their loyalty and to attract others. Sometimes the business model continues to involve assessments but often the alliance begins supplying a product or service. The business model must be based on meeting the needs of the people and organizations it serves. For example, in a trade association, the members must obtain value for their dues. In a standards development organization, the key is consistency among subscribers—if there aren't enough subscriber dues to make the effort sustainable, the alliance fails.

Self-Perpetuating Corporate Governance

In a non-enterprise alliance, when the effort is concluded, the leadership disbands. In an alliance enterprise, the group must establish a governance structure as the original conveners and leaders withdraw. An alliance enterprise is a special-purpose private democracy. People join and remain voluntarily, agreeing to abide by the conditions established. This special-purpose private democracy needs the capacity to elect those who govern and lead.

VARIOUS FORMS OF ALLIANCE ENTERPRISE

Alliance enterprises are everywhere. Agricultural cooperatives have been formed for centuries to share equipment and facilitate marketing, processing, or purchasing. Trade associations cover nearly every industry sector, formed when businesses with common problems create formal entities to advance their collective interests. Intergovernmental entities are established to manage multijurisdictional problems. Public (government) and private (businesses) entities form alliance enterprises like GEOSS or the Grand Canyon Visibility Transport Commission or Western Governors University to accomplish a specific task no one entity can achieve alone. Standards organizations have emerged to maintain and govern standards on matters as diverse as the rules of a sport or the interoperability of electronic medical records. Universities jointly create a service to manage enrollment processes so students need to fill out the paperwork only once for multiple institutions. Homeowners associations are established to manage common areas within a neighborhood. Irrigation companies exist to manage scarce water resources. Electricity and natural gas companies form power exchange organizations and pipelines to share energy. Group purchasing organizations deliver economies of scale and efficiency to buyers and sellers.

Alliance enterprises also exist within organizations. For instance, a health care services company found that while new sales were brisk, its people were struggling to implement their services efficiently. After investigating the cause of the inefficiency, it discovered that it had two poorly coordinated functions. Finger-pointing between the departments created an unhealthy tension that only exacerbated the problem. The CEO convened a day-long session to sort the problem out. As a result of that meeting, leaders determined an ongoing collaboration was necessary to provide a higher level of customer service. The company established a permanent council to integrate delivery of services between the functions. Though they might have tried to handle the problem informally or with a temporary alliance, the managers realized that anything less than a permanent, semi-independent group would only be able to put a bandage on problems. The organization required continuous oversight of the two functions by a semiautonomous entity that would establish its own rules, governance, and methods of solving the problem.

Unlike temporary value alliances, alliance enterprises require an ongoing organization to facilitate collaboration. When alliances segue from a temporary to a permanent entity, they benefit by incorporating the following factors:

Lower costs and shared risk. Over time, reduced costs and risks add up to significant savings. Members of alliance enterprises need to achieve these savings over time. While they may not be significant in the short term, in the long term they can help all member businesses run much more cost-efficiently and minimize problems in a downturn. When the cost of a necessary process or service is shared among the many over time, the unit cost for member organizations becomes lower. For example, airlines in an alliance can funnel passengers from one airline to another based on occupied seats—this helps airlines avoid the cost of empty seats (especially on long international flights). Similarly, ten businesses in noncompeting markets join an alliance enterprise so they can give a manufacturer one large order, gaining volume discounts they would not qualify for on their own. Again, this solves an ongoing problem—over the course of five or ten years, the savings may make a major difference in terms of profit and sustainability.

Improved perspective. Many organizations find that the problems they face grow more intractable and complex by the year. Despite the large size of some of these organizations, they recognize their perspective is limited by their culture and training. To deal with confusing, challenging problems in the coming years, they know they will require the diverse ideas that alliance enterprises provide. When multidiscipline groups work on a problem, they see the problem from more points of view and hence can create more potential solutions.

Specialization efficiency. To solve some ongoing problems, organizations require a degree of specialization that often isn't possible in a single entity. Alliance enterprises make it possible to link experts in ways that make them more effective at solving problems that will surface for many years to come. For example, executives of the New York Yankees baseball team and Dallas Cowboys football team formed an alliance enterprise called Legends Hospitality Management to manage the concessions at their respective ballparks.[1] Because of its inherent scale and expertise, the enterprise has since been hired by other professional sports teams.

Independent validation. Nonprofit entities are often created to provide independent validation within an industry. Recognizing that such validation will be crucial not just to solve one problem but for a variety of problems over a long stretch of time, conveners in these industries organize validation-focused alliance enterprises. For example, in India, spices are an important national export. However, the producers know that one adverse health incident because of poor quality or contamination could damage the entire Indian spice trade. An alliance enterprise called the Spice Board was created. It is governed by the industry and government jointly and its mission is to collaboratively promote quality and marketing. It has developed a certification process that allows producers of spices to offer their customers assurance that the product has been produced according to independently validated best practices.[2]

In a world of intensifying competition, where survival requires finding ways to continually enhance productivity, the use of alliance enterprises will become an increasingly important tool. Certainly value alliances of limited duration will have their place as targeted problem-solving tools, but a new, ongoing collaborative structure will become increasingly necessary. In the past an organization's success was rarely dependent on others. In the future success is likely to be determined, at least in part, by the alliance enterprises organizations form or join.

EVOLVING BEYOND ORIGINAL CONCEPT

Most alliance enterprises are created to solve a problem, but they often evolve into serious, ongoing businesses. In 2000, then GE Healthcare head Jeff Immelt and Group Chairman Kirk Selquist of J&J's Healthcare Systems discovered they shared a problem. Both companies serve the health care field and they could see the marketplace changing in a way that threatened the customer contact and service model of their enterprises. New supply exchanges had begun to develop that would insert themselves as go-betweens in the manufacturer-customer relationship, with the goal of charging a toll for their services. Immelt and Selquist recognized that if these exchanges obtained a strong foothold, they would add complexity to conducting business, increase the cost of products sold by GE, J&J, and other health care companies, and probably be difficult to dislodge. Immelt and Selquist convened an alliance enterprise called Global Healthcare Exchange (GHX), which was joined by other leading health care companies.

GHX was initially staffed by executives on loan from the companies that founded it. While its original purpose was to prevent unjustified cost increases, it expanded to take a significantly greater role in the industry. As it became clear that it provided a value-added solution to a common problem, GHX attracted major health care businesses that shared the conveners' concerns. Abbott Labs, Baxter, Medtronic, Siemens, and others soon declared their willingness to participate.

The participants made financial investments in the new alliance. A permanent management team was hired and offices established, and GHX began the process of creating an exchange large enough to discourage others from escalating costs. Over the next few years, it built a highly leveraged network resource, automating key procedures and driving out unnecessary supply chain transaction costs. It made major acquisitions of similar health care supply exchanges that had been started by group purchasing organizations and other groups to achieve a dominant position. With a central hub of information for a rapidly growing membership base (including more than four thousand hospitals, health care product suppliers, group purchasing organizations, and others), GHX's shared electronic network not only saved members money but improved processing time and accuracy. In fact, GHX estimates it has saved the industry over $3 billion and has become the health care industry's clearinghouse for processing supply orders and invoices. Clearly, GHX has evolved beyond the conveners' original vision, and it continues to evolve in new directions.[3]

When HHS set out to encourage the development of uniform standards for interoperability among electronic medical records (EMR), the American Health Information Community was formed to develop those standards collaboratively. As the standards began to emerge, we had another problem—how to certify EMR systems that complied with the standards. We felt strongly that certifying systems for compliance was not a good role for government so we encouraged the development of an alliance enterprise called the Certification Commission on Health Information Technology (CCHIT).

The conveners for CCHIT were three important and respected health information technology nonprofits. They launched a limited alliance to plan the creation of a permanent entity. Once the plan was accepted by their respective boards of directors, CCHIT was formed in 2004. It began with governance process and business plans and was funded by grants from HHS, but within three years it had to develop a sustainable business model using fees charged EMR developers to test and judge if their products would meet the standards.[4]

Later, this process was enhanced when the government adopted a requirement that health care providers must demonstrate that they made meaningful use of the standard capacities required for compliance.

Without the contributions of CCHIT as an alliance enterprise, this process would have been difficult to achieve.

ALLIANCE ENTERPRISES ARE THE FUTURE . . . AND INCREASINGLY, THE PRESENT

While cooperative enterprises have always existed, the globalized nature of the emerging culture and the capacity to be connected through technology have produced an environment where joining, forming, and sustaining the right alliance enterprises will be essential for success in every arena—business, nonprofit, government, and elsewhere. Joining or forming a limited-time alliance will be something most leaders and organizations will do with increasing frequency, and these alliances will provide great value and even greater experience at working collaboratively.

The real challenge, though, is becoming part of an alliance that lasts. Whether you turn your limited-time alliance into an enterprise or join an alliance designed to exist for many years, this group may help you solve numerous problems and by extension capitalize on numerous opportunities. It will be the type of alliance that offers enormous problem-solving capacity to its members year after year after year.

TWELVE

Collaborative Competitive Edge

Once sensitized to the existence of value alliances, you will begin to see them everywhere. In fact, most businesses and organizations are typically engaged in discussions about several potential collaborations at any given moment. In the coming years, this number will undoubtedly increase due to a confluence of four key trends: digitization, transportation technology, geopolitical expansion of market-based economies, and the pressure of mounting sovereign debt within industrialized economies. Individually, each of these factors causes the number of collaborative alliances to increase. Collectively, they represent a new platform for productivity enhancement.

VIRTUOUS CYCLE OF COLLABORATIVE COMPETITION

A virtuous cycle is at work here. The more collaborative networks improve productivity, the more important collaborative skills become to achieving success in the marketplace. As the four key trends gain traction, they will make the need for collaborative intelligence (CI) even greater in upcoming years than it is today.

Digital Technology

The Internet has created the capacity to simply and routinely tie geographically disparate components of a network together, making businesses on different continents and under different ownership part of the same just-in-time supply chain. With more and more processes disaggregated and outsourced with mass-customized precision, vertical integration becomes less attractive. "Big data" or "data warehouses" and "cloud computing" allow massive amounts of data to be aggregated and sliced and diced in ways that find and exploit smaller and smaller increments of productivity. This connectedness on its own will compel the creation of ever more collaborative alliances.

For instance, a careful examination of the business model of all the major consulting organizations—such as Deloitte, Pricewaterhouse Coopers, and Ernst & Young—reveals that while they represent themselves under a common global brand, they are really formal business alliances of independent enterprises. Yes, they have a common name that ties them together as a brand, but the vast majority of their operation involves local profit centers and ownership. The ownership of the China operation is different from the ownership of the U.S. operation, for example. The worldwide CEO of one of the big four explained to me that they can no longer be competitive on large contracts inside the United States without having more than 50 percent of the work done in India, China, or Vietnam. Every contract is a collaborative alliance among in-house participants.

This isn't a trend limited to large businesses. Exchanges like Odesk .com bring together purchasers and providers of services as allies in an international marketplace. A small nonprofit outsources its video editing to a Romanian business, for example, at a cost less than 5 percent of what it would be inside the United States. A U.S. organization has accountants in India who were trained in the United States and can work for less than $5 per hour. More and more collaborative alliances are being assembled across international borders because of digitization.

Standardized Transportation Systems

The advent and scaling of standardized shipping technologies dramatically lowers the cost of moving goods around the globe. When combined with digital technology, this allows high-level innovation skills to be complemented by inexpensive labor. Virtually every supply chain now includes components that are assembled in different countries and then combined in still another global location. I recently bought a new golfing sand wedge. The club was designed in the United States but the shaft was made in China and the club head was forged in India. The assembly took place in Mexico. Every part of that club was shipped through a matrix of standardized shipping container systems. Ordering of each component part was managed by a digital network, controlling the inventory of all four enterprises. Systems like this among suppliers aren't purchased off the shelf. They result from common pain (or opportunity) assuaged by good convening, committed leadership, and common standard development.

Geopolitical Changes

In the past two decades, governments with planned economies have embraced market principles and encouraged the expansion of global trading relationships. China, Vietnam, and Russia are three notable examples. Other less developed market economies like India and Brazil have also become prominent. Value alliances are an expression of market-based principles playing out. As market activity increases, so does competition. With competition comes an imperative to produce goods and services of better quality at lower costs. As global competition intensifies, collaboration skills become vital for survival.

Economic Realities of Sovereign Debt

Currently much of the developed world struggles to manage large accumulations of sovereign debt. In the United States, Europe, and other leading economies, expenditures have exceeded revenues for lengthy periods of time. This creates a higher collective level of common pain. To illustrate this principle, here is a tale that may seem tangential at first but ultimately provides an impactful lesson.

When I became governor of Utah, my family and I moved into a beautiful and historic home traditionally referred to as the Governor's Mansion. Less than a year later, at Christmastime, a state maintenance team improperly wired a Christmas tree and a terrible fire broke out. Fortunately, our family escaped. We were huddled on the lawn of a neighboring building when the windows in the mansion suddenly exploded and flames shot out.

The following day I walked through the charred home with the State Fire Marshall. I asked him about the dramatic explosion. He explained that within a matter of seconds the fire had burned all the oxygen from the home. The lack of oxygen created a vacuum that sucked the windows out of their frames. Then, the flames jumped toward the source of new oxygen.

To further illustrate the principle, the Fire Marshall took a screw driver from his pocket and lifted the cover of a light switch. As he withdrew the first screw he showed me signs of smoke and heat damage. He said, "When fire is looking for oxygen, it looks everywhere—including under the screws of the light switch. It's a natural survival instinct."

When national governments dramatically reduce spending or run out of money, it creates an effect much like a fire running out of oxygen. Whether it's oxygen or money, when something essential for survival starts to disappear, the search begins for a fresh source. For many organizations, this search entails seeking new levels of productivity.

In a money-deprived environment, spending must be curtailed or taxes increased or a combination of both. The pressure is on to find value in new ways. Collaboration offers various groups an innovative method to decrease costs and increase productivity.

CHOOSING ALLIANCES WISELY

As a consequence of the four trends discussed here, the future prosperity of most enterprises will be affected by their ability to select allies and decide which alliances to join or form. Failure in alliance building can be expensive in economic terms and disastrous strategically. Knowing which alliances have the best prospects of success should be viewed as an investment decision. This is true for alliances formed to solve specific problems or those that involve long-term business relationships. The eight key elements of a successful value alliance can also serve as criteria to help you assess an invitation to participate in forming or joining a value alliance:

Common Pain

All the collaborators in a value alliance must have sufficient motivation to make the effort, expense, and occasional aggravation worthwhile. Will each of the participants have a reason to go the distance? If you are invited to participate in solving a problem collaboratively, the first question to ask is whether it has sufficient value for you. If it doesn't, obviously, you won't join. However, if it is worthwhile for you, that doesn't mean a proposed alliance meets the common pain test. You need to examine the motivation of all the participants, especially those you deem critical to success. If you can't understand why they want to participate, ask them. Until you can understand the value of participation to all involved, remain skeptical.

Convener of Stature

In collaborative problem solving the behavior of the participants will in large measure be driven by the environment of trust and reliability created by the convener. When evaluating your participation in a value alliance, make an assessment of the commitment and skill of the conveners and determine if you think they can assemble the group and manage it in a way that will produce success. If not, save your time, capital, and ideas. In the GHX example, the backing of two of America's leading corporations (GE and Johnson & Johnson) demonstrated to all representatives the sustainability of the coalition. It reassured them that the Alliance was built to last.

Representatives of Substance

To make a wise investment, evaluate who will be representing each of the participants in the value alliance. If important parties are sending junior people who lack authority or stature within their organization, the alliance is likely to fail or have little impact. If a key company or individual is missing, that absence sows doubt about the Alliance's future.

In the Surescripts example, leaders of both major sectors of the industry joined, demonstrating to everyone that this alliance had legs. CCHIT, too, had not only the leaders of the three most important trade groups in the EMR world, but a clear institutional buy-in. When GEOSS was formed, the key industrialized nations that had the economic capacity to support this effort were at the table; high-ranking officials from all these nations also participated. This signaled to other countries that this was a sustainable and serious-minded effort.

Committed Leader

We have all been in meetings where there was no clear leader. Collaboration among parties with various interests is difficult at the best of times. Without an appointed and acknowledged leader, alliances are rarely efficient and often unsuccessful. Before you agree to participate in a value alliance, evaluate the leadership structure or the method of choosing the leader. If you do not see skilled and clear leadership, either assume that task yourself or stay away.

Clearly Defined Purpose

Uncertain or generalized missions are the enemy of most would-be value alliances. Before agreeing to join an alliance, assess whether it has a clearly defined purpose. Ask yourself whether all members of the group see the objective similarly. If members are really there for different purposes that make the group's purpose too broad or unachievable, your participation is unlikely to be worthwhile.

When we organized the American Health Information Committee, we knew that if we defined our purpose broadly and generally—say, as creating standards for health information technology—it would be impossible to achieve such an ambitious objective. To avoid this failure, we identified clearly defined priorities and outcomes.

With an alliance enterprise, potential participants naturally worry that the mission of the organization could expand to areas where the alliance becomes their own organization's competitor. What you should be looking for here, then, is language that indicates the purpose is not going to expand into your turf. You also want to make sure that this purpose is as long range as it is narrow—that the alliance is designed for the long term.

A Formal Charter

In evaluating whether to join a collaborative alliance you will want to read any documents describing the work plan for clues on how well organized the effort is likely to be. However, most often organizers of alliances have not written a charter. This is a contribution you can make that will improve the operation and likelihood of success. A critical element in the charter is the method of decision making. Consensus decision making encourages open discussion, active listening, and a search for right answers. The charter should specify that the governance process—including the method of selecting a governing board if one is contemplated—must be carried out in a balanced and fair way. You don't want to invest in an alliance that is going to become the tool of a single organization or individual (or a small, powerful group). Instead, you want to invest when the Charter provides for an equitable means of governance.

The Northbound Train

In a limited-purpose alliance, evaluate whether you and others believe the outcome will be positive. If you doubt the mission as it has been described can be achieved, don't waste your time and money pursuing it. In an alliance enterprise, emphasis shifts to the value proposition and brand of the new entity. This means that the alliance must develop a strong, consistent reputation for providing value to its members. It's not just about generating optimism that the alliance can accomplish a single objective but that it will provide value to members year after year. These attributes are important to attract and maintain a critical mass of participation.

Creating the northbound train is especially important when more than one alliance enterprise will be competing for the same purpose. Recall that CCHIT had its beginning as part of an effort at HHS to create a testing and certification organization to determine if electronic medical record systems adequately incorporated national standards. HHS offered a large grant as an incentive to the organization that produced the best plan. Initially, many trade associations and groups made proposals. However, as the competition heated up, leading organizations realized they could make a better offering if they formed a collaborative alliance. As a result, organizations looked to join the alliance that seemed like it was the northbound train.

Common Assumptions

Part of evaluating the likelihood of success of any alliance is whether the group can agree upon some basic beginning points. For example, if an alliance includes parties from North, Central, and South America, should participants assume they're going to be speaking English or Spanish in meetings? Will they measure distances in meters or yards? Are they going to meet monthly or quarterly? Part of your investment analysis should be whether these questions have been discussed and the likelihood of agreement. If you find out these core issues have not been discussed, that should be a red flag. If they have been discussed but no agreement was reached—that is equally worrisome.

In evaluating your participation, think through what the most difficult disagreement might be and assess if the group is likely to break down in trying to reach consensus on it. If that is true, success is unlikely.

In the world of computer software, some groups feel the best way to succeed is to build products with an open source. This means anyone can have access to the source code, helping create new and better products more quickly. Others believe a proprietary interest should be maintained to control quality and enhance profits. It is important to choose alliance partners who share a philosophy you believe to be best and most sustainable. If the objective was to build a successful alliance among organizations with different philosophies on this question, it would be well not to squander resources working together unless and until this key assumption is settled.

CONCLUSION

A TIME FOR GREAT COLLABORATIONS

The opportunities to collaborate are numerous and multiplying, but capitalizing on them requires reliance on a structured and disciplined methodology. In this book we outline an adaptable framework of eight key criteria that must exist for successful collaborative efforts—criteria that can also be used to evaluate invitations you receive to participate in such efforts. While collaboration has always existed, this book is devoted to the proposition that collaboration is a skill or competency that can be improved with study, practice, and experience, and that current business environments dictate that now is the time when honing this skill is essential.

It is useful to look at some of the trends and forces that are making effective collaboration so crucial to so many different organizations. First, though, we want to emphasize that we're referring to a very specific collaborative approach. We have introduced the term *value alliance* as a means of distinguishing a formalized collaborative entity from ad hoc efforts. The former is necessary to optimize results. Good collaboration is not a casual undertaking. It requires effort, leadership, structure, process, and commitment. While we did not invent the concept of formalizing collaborative efforts, we have identified the elements required for success through extensive testing in a wide variety of settings and fields.

KEY TRENDS

Value alliances are needed in just about every type of endeavor to solve a staggering range of problems. Here are some of the fields and forces driving the creation of value alliances:

Health Care

The United States struggles under the weight of high health care costs and social program commitments like Medicare, Medicaid, and new Affordable Care Act subsidies. The future burden of these obligations represents a threat to the competitiveness of American workers and their employers. Many economists worry that if this trend continues, interest rates on sovereign debt will spike—adding to the deficit and making it even more difficult to make the investments necessary for the United States to maintain its current economic leadership.

In response to this problem, health care payers (insurers, governments, and employers) have begun to demand price reductions from physicians, hospitals, and the various medical service providers. They have also begun to change the basic model of compensation used to pay those rendering care. Rather than paying separately for each procedure, medication dose, device, or service (a process called fee-for-service billing), groups of medical providers are paid a specific sum of money to assume responsibility for the health care of large groups of people. Those operating under this new approach are collectively referred to as Accountable Care Organizations, often referenced as ACOs. Success in this new model of care and payment will be largely determined by the effectiveness of hospitals, doctors, nursing homes, and service providers working collaboratively together to provide the best care at a low cost.

In our consulting practice we have a team tracking the development progress of hundreds of ACOs. Nearly all have similar problems. There are issues with technology compatibility, challenges deciding how much each provider will be paid, and disagreements over how medical and financial decisions will be made. All these decisions require a level of collaboration never required before in health care. This need for heightened collaborative intelligence is not limited to senior health care executives working to navigate their enterprise through this new environment—individual caregivers at the nurses' station need it just as much. Routinely we find that the biggest obstacle to success isn't the technology, the governance, or the economic model but rather the sociology of getting people to find aligned interests. This is where the formation of a value alliance with the eight key elements discussed here will provide significant benefits.

National Security

National security in the United States and other nations will depend on more effective collaboration among the various branches of the military, intelligence-gathering entities, and allies around the world. General Stanley McChrystal told us of the challenge faced by U.S. forces in Iraq and Afghanistan when he arrived as commander. They confronted an enemy who was less well equipped than U.S. forces but operated as a network (al Qaida), constantly changing tactics to take advantage of the siloed, top-down structure of the U.S. military. His conclusion—"You need to be a network to defeat a network"—not only paved the way to U.S. resurgence in those two theaters but has also become a twenty-first-century war doctrine. Military forces are redefining themselves to become more collaborative. For generations branches of the U.S. military operated in the strict silos of Army, Navy, Air Force, Marines, and Coast Guard. Now, it is not uncommon to hear people speak of the "purple force," a reference to the outcome of blending the colors of the various military branches.

Not only has the nature of the enemy faced by the military changed to become more networked, the economic pressures on the military to be more collaborative have grown. Collaboration and the creation of value alliances across service lines has become a requirement to keep our nation safe.

Product Safety and Supply Chains

Among the executives of a large retail chain, the phrase "speed is life" defines a critical part of their culture. The ability to act quickly and decisively with a minimum of deliberation and discussion is a critical component of their capacity to deliver a product to their customers at the lowest possible price. For that reason just-in-time inventory systems have become an essential component of economic competitiveness. The development process to organize a just-in-time system often constitutes a value alliance with various participants collaboratively working through the challenge of delivering component parts to a factory or sales floor, "just in time."

A similar force is operating in the food and drug industry. Companies in this sector in both the United States and other countries face new product safety rules and regulations, catalyzing the development of new standards. This can only be done well if collaboration is the platform.

Environmental Problem Solving

Our stewardship of the environment is often in conflict with our need for energy and other natural resources. There are other conflicts as well, such as our desire for clear air, water, and land conflicting with need for housing, recreation, and business growth. This book contains multiple examples of value alliances that provided a platform to find the golden mean necessary to provide for both preservation and development. As resources become more precious and our population changes, collaborative skills provide a pathway to resolve the conflicts.

Science and Technology

Collaborative science is a new frontier of discovery. A significant percentage of the grant applications submitted at the National Institutes of Health and other scientific organizations include collaborative efforts from different universities, scientists with different disciplines of training, or both. The value alliance structure described in this book provides a platform to increase the productivity of such efforts.

Public Policy and Advocacy

When people of a common mind feel aggrieved by a threatened policy or legal outcome, alliances form. Coalitions of independent parties initiate joint efforts to defend or achieve a legislative or community goal. Unfortunately, many of these efforts are messy and unorganized. The eight key elements of a value alliance, on the other hand, provide efficiencies and organization that increase the likelihood of success.

COLLABORATION AND FREEDOM

One aspect of collaboration is rarely acknowledged as a critical component: freedom and self-governance. During my service in President Bush's cabinet, a government official from a communist nation taught me an important lesson about democracy and capitalism. We sat together at dinner after a long day of negotiating a sensitive matter. We began to talk about our different forms of government. His nation was doing its best to move from a centrally planned economy toward a market system within the framework of a nondemocratic government. I complained that his nation's system had too much regulation and that I thought it made collaboration difficult. I suggested it inhibited the capacity to innovate.

My friend responded by offering a challenge of his own. "You Americans," he said, "think that if a nation holds an election it can begin functioning like a democracy. What you fail to understand about your own country is that it has a two-hundred-year heritage of moral values based on a belief in God. That belief compels people to do the right thing because of an accountability they feel. As a result, most people voluntarily abide by the law and pay their taxes. You started as a capitalist system. You have codes of ethics and regulations and laws that have been refined over time. You have a culture that was made for collaboration and innovation.

"Our system is based on the ideal that the government would define the rules and regulate all behavior. We are trying to change. But it's going to take time."

My friend the communist leader taught me two things that night. First, that trust facilitates collaboration and innovation. Second, the secret sauce of a capitalist society is the ability to develop trust based on traditions of moral behavior.

When trust is present, collaboration runs smoothly; people are open and in problem-solving mode. When trust is absent, the gears of collaboration are slow and grinding. Time is spent in unproductive suspicion, drama, and repeated validation. Freedom is the trust a society grants itself. It fosters collaboration and innovation. Heavy regulation represents the distrust society imposes on itself, and it stifles collaboration and innovation.

Free societies possess this competitive advantage in the global marketplace. The value alliance concept will help them keep and strengthen it.

To help keep and strengthen this advantage, we intend to start a dialogue about allies, alliances, and collaboration. The lessons you've learned from your participation in collaborative entities (big, small, and in between) can inform, expand, and improve our individual and collective thinking. We invite you to join us in the ongoing conversation hosted at findingallies.com. We look forward to reading about your experiences.

APPENDIX

WRAP CHARTER

Approved December 2009

This statement sets forth the purposes, principles and operating procedures for the Western Regional Air Partnership (WRAP).

PURPOSES

The WRAP provides a venue for Western states, tribes, local air agencies, federal land managers and the USEPA to:

1. Maintain and update the regional haze work that WRAP has developed and continue to make the data and tools available for states and tribes to use as they implement their regional haze implementation plans;
2. Develop a common understanding of current and evolving regional air quality issues in the West, such as regional haze, ozone, fine and coarse particulate matter, nitrogen deposition and critical loads, and mercury and other hazardous air pollutants;
3. Examine and discuss Western regional air quality issues from a multi-pollutant perspective;

4. Develop and maintain regional databases that support regional and sub-regional technical analyses. This includes collection and analysis of data from various sources to produce regionally consistent, comparable, complete, and transparent results, able to be utilized and relied upon by individual jurisdictions and agencies;

5. Collaborate with USEPA to ensure that, to the maximum extent possible, WRAP data and analyses are compatible with and leverage work conducted at the national level. This could include WRAP work to compile data and analyses related to international, off-shore, and other sources of air pollution affecting Western air quality;

6. Evaluate the air quality impacts associated with regionally significant emission sources, such as mobile sources, fire, traditional and alternative energy development/extraction, windblown dust, and electricity generation, and, as warranted, to discuss regional and cross-jurisdictional strategies to improve air quality and mitigate the impacts from such sources;

7. Consult with air quality agencies in other regions to reduce duplication of effort and enhance efficiency and consistency of databases and analyses;

8. Evaluate how the impacts of climate change may affect air quality in the West; and

9. As requested by the membership, formulate and advance consensus positions on Western regional air quality issues.

PRINCIPLES

The WRAP is a voluntary partnership of states, tribes, local air agencies, federal land managers and USEPA. The Partnership recognizes the unique legal status and jurisdiction of tribes and seeks to promote policies that ensure fair and equitable treatment of all participating members of the WRAP. The Partnership also recognizes state, tribal and local air agency authority and responsibility to develop, adopt, and implement individual air quality plans within their jurisdictions.[1]

Further, the Partnership recognizes the role of the U.S. Environmental Protection Agency and its responsibility to develop national regulatory initiatives, review and approve State and Tribal implementation plans, and develop Federal implementation plans as necessary. In addition, the Partnership recognizes the affirmative responsibility of the federal land management agencies under the Clean Air Act to protect the air quality related values, including visibility at mandatory Class I federal areas and to manage all the areas under their respective jurisdictions for the public purposes set forth in their governing statutory authorities.

The WRAP has no regulatory authority and recognizes that all legal authority is reserved by its members in accordance with existing law. The Partnership also recognizes the United States' trust responsibility as carried out by the federal agencies to protect tribal resources from degradation.

As a voluntary partnership, the WRAP is formed as an organization exempt from the Federal Advisory Committee Act. The WRAP will conduct its processes consistent with the concepts of open and participatory government.

OPERATING PROCEDURES

Membership

Membership in the WRAP is open to all states, federally recognized tribes, and local air agencies located in the geographical region encompassed by the states of: Alaska, Arizona, California, Colorado, Hawaii, Idaho, Montana, Nevada, New Mexico, North Dakota, Oregon, South Dakota, Utah, Washington, and Wyoming.

Membership in the WRAP is also open to the U.S. Forest Service, National Park Service, Bureau of Land Management, Fish and Wildlife Service, and U.S. EPA.

In order to become a recognized member of the WRAP, eligible states, tribes, local air agencies, and federal agencies shall submit an official letter to the WRAP requesting membership and designating primary and secondary contacts for the jurisdiction or agency.[2]

Any tribe in the WRAP region may participate in the WRAP; however, for membership/Board matters brought to a vote, recognized membership is needed.

Board of Directors

The WRAP Members shall establish a Board of Directors consisting of five state, five tribal, five federal, and two local air agency representatives. The state, tribal, and local directors shall be elected by their respective delegations to staggered two-year terms, with the option for directors to be re-elected to additional terms. The directors representing eligible federal agencies shall be appointed by their agencies to two-year terms with the option of extension at the option of the respective agencies.

Alternates
A Board member may designate an alternate from their jurisdiction or agency to represent them at a meeting of the Board by notifying the co-chairs in writing three days prior to the meeting.

Officers
The officers of WRAP shall consist of: a) two Co-Chairs—one being a state government representative and one being a tribal government representative; b) a Treasurer; and c) a Secretary. Officers shall be elected from among the membership of the Board of Directors by a majority vote of the Board.

Duties of Officers
The WRAP Co-Chairpersons shall develop agendas for and jointly preside at all WRAP membership meetings and meetings of the Board of Directors and shall facilitate consensus on all issues that come before the organization.

The WRAP Secretary shall create a written summary of WRAP membership and board meetings and transmit this information to all members of WRAP.

The WRAP Treasurer shall produce quarterly financial statements and propose budgets to the members of WRAP.

Powers of WRAP Board

In directing the activities of the WRAP, the Board of Directors may:

- Solicit and accept funding;
- Hire staff, or arrange for the provision of staff support, to carry out its activities;
- Approve work plans;
- Approve contracts for support from outside experts and consultants;
- Establish a Technical Steering Committee from the membership to oversee and direct the technical and analytical work of WRAP staff, contractors, and work groups;
- Establish Work Groups from the membership to manage specific elements of the work plan; and
- Call membership meetings.

Quorums

A quorum at meetings and conference calls of the Board of Directors shall be representation from two-thirds of the current members of the Board.

Meetings of the Board of Directors

The WRAP Board of Directors shall hold an annual meeting each year but may meet as often as is necessary to conduct its business. Business shall only be conducted in the presence of a quorum. All decisions whether by voting or consensus shall require a quorum.

All meetings of the Board of Directors, whether in-person or via teleconference, shall be open to the membership (including an option to participate for members to participate via teleconference) and conducted according to Robert's Rules of Order. Minutes of the meeting and other status or program reports shall be made available to the public as appropriate determined by the Board of Directors.

The WRAP Board shall provide the membership with at least 15 day's prior notice of its meetings. The notice shall indicate the time, date, place and purpose of the meeting and include a summary of the agenda. Meetings shall be held at a reasonable time, and in a place reasonably accessible to the membership. The Co-Chairpersons shall submit to all members of the Board of Directors any matter being proposed for a vote no fewer than ten days in advance of the meeting at which the vote is scheduled to be taken.

Consensus and Issue Resolution

It is the intent of the WRAP Board to resolve all issues on a consensus (general agreement) basis. Whenever there is disagreement among Board members, each member must commit to making all reasonable efforts to achieve consensus.

The WRAP Board may vote on administrative matters when consensus cannot be reached on such issues. Administrative matters include the election of officers, budget adoption and other issues related to the general management of the organization. A vote for determining whether a matter is of an administrative nature requires the support of two-thirds of the Board members present. Passage of any matter on which a vote is taken requires the support of a majority of the Board members present. When consensus cannot be reached, positions of members may be recorded for purposes of the public record.

Stakeholder Participation

The WRAP Board of Directors shall be responsible for ensuring appropriate stakeholder participation in its process. This shall include: 1) ensuring that meetings of the WRAP membership are open to the public; 2) providing opportunities for stakeholder review and comment on WRAP products; and 3) approving participation in WRAP technical work groups by non-members who have particular expertise in a given subject area such that their participation is likely to improve the quality of the work being conducted.

Charter Amendments

This charter may be amended by a two-thirds vote of the current membership of the organization, with each member state, tribe, local air agency, and federal agency having one vote. Amendments to the charter shall be introduced 14 days prior to any vote to amend the charter.

NOTES

Chapter 1

1. "History of Visa." Visa. Available online: http://corporate.visa.com/about -visa/our-business/history-of-visa.shtml. Accessed March 20, 2013.

2. "How the EU Works: 1957." European Union, n.d. Available online: http:// europa.eu/about-eu/eu-history/1945-1959/1957/index_en.htm. Accessed March 20, 2013.

3. "What Is NATO?" NATO, n.d. Available online: www.nato.int/nato -welcome/index.html. Accessed April 20, 2013.

4. Woolf, S. H., and Laudan, A. *U.S. Health in International Perspective: Shorter Lives, Poorer Health* (Washington DC: National Academies Press, 2013).

5. Presidential Documents: "Executive Order 13335." U.S. Government Printing Office, April 27, 2004. Available online: www.gpo.gov/fdsys/pkg /FR-2004-04-30/pdf/04-10024.pdf. Accessed April 20, 2013. Also based on Rich McKeown, personal interview with Kerry Weems, September 21, 2012.

6. Bowen, C. D. *Miracle at Philadelphia: The Story of the Constitutional Convention* (Boston: Back Bay Books, 1966), p. 36.

7. "Higher Education: Not What It Used to Be." *Economist*, December 1, 2012. Available online: www.economist.com/news/united-states/21567373 -american-universities-represent-declining-value-money-their-students-not -what-it. Accessed April 19, 2013.

8. "Enrollment Reaches 36,000 Students." Western Governors University, October 18, 2012. Available online: www.wgu.edu/about_WGU/enroll ment_reaches_36000_10-18-12. Accessed 4/20/13.

9. "A History of SkyTeam." Breaking Travel News, July 27, 2001. Available online: www.breakingtravelnews.com/news/article/btn40002875/. Accessed June 28, 2012.

Chapter 2

1. The Papers of George Washington Documents. See Henry Knox to GW, 23 October. ALS (photocopy), CSmH; LB, DLC:GW. The ALS was reported sold in the *New York Times*, 7 Dec. 1892. From "The Papers," Confederation Series 4:331-332. Available online: http://gwpapers.virginia.edu/documents /constitution/1784/madison2.html. Accessed April 20, 2013.

2. Niles, R. "Eclipse Files for Bankruptcy Protection." Avweb, November 25, 2008. Available online: www.avweb.com/avwebflash/news/EclipseAviation _Chaper11Bankruptcy_199283-1.html. Accessed April 19, 2013.

3. "About Eclipse 500 Club." Eclipse Owners Club, n.d. Available online: www.eclipse500club.org/about/. Accessed April 19, 2013.

4. "Company Background." GHX, 2013. Available online: www.ghx.com /about-ghx/company-background.aspx. Accessed April 20, 2013.

5. "Global Earth Observation System of Systems (GEOSS)." U.S. Department of Commerce, National Oceanic and Atmospheric Administration, n.d. Available online: www.publicaffairs.noaa.gov/budget2006/pdf/geoss2006 .pdf. Accessed April 20, 2013.

6. Schmidt, J. O., Blum, M. S., and Overal, W. L. "Hemolytic Activities of Stinging Insect Venoms," *Archives of Insect Biochemistry and Physiology* 1 (1984): 155–160.

Chapter 3

1. "Clinton Health Access Initiative." Clinton Foundation, n.d. Available online: www.clintonfoundation.org/main/our-work/by-initiative/clinton -health-access-initiative/about.html. Accessed March 20, 2013.

2. "Drafting the Great Lakes Regional Collaboration Strategy to Restore and Protect the Great Lakes." Great Lakes Regional Collaboration, August 22, 2007. Available online: http://glrc.us/process.html. Accessed April 20, 2013.

Chapter 4

1. "History." Lloyd's of London, 2013. Available online: www.lloyds.com /lloyds/about-us/history. Accessed April 20, 2013.

2. "American Health Information Community: Overview." IT Law Wiki, n.d. Available online: http://itlaw.wikia.com/wiki/American_Health _Information_Community. Accessed April 20, 2013.

Chapter 5

1. "IFTA: Articles of Agreement." International Fuel Tax Association, January 2010. Available online: www.iftach.org/manuals/2010/AA/Articles%20of%20 Agreement%20FINAL%20-%20January%202010.pdf. Accessed April 20, 2013.

Chapter 6

1. "IFTA: Articles of Agreement." International Fuel Tax Association, January 2010. Available online: www.iftach.org/manuals/2010/AA/Articles%20 of%20Agreement%20FINAL%20-%20January%202010.pdf. Accessed April 20, 2013.

2. Hayosh, Thomas D. "The History of the Check and Standardization Efforts," September 26, 1995. Available online: http://home.comcast .net/~hayosh/HISTMICR.pdf. Accessed May 2, 2013.

3. "Global Earth Observation System of Systems (GEOSS) and the Group on Earth Observations (GEO)." U.S. Environmental Protection Agency, n.d. Available online: www.epa.gov/geoss/. Accessed April 20, 2013.

4. Rich McKeown, interview with Bill Carlson, former vice president, GHX, June 25, 2012. See also "Company Background." GHX, 2013. Available online: www.ghx.com/about-ghx/company-background.aspx. Accessed May 2, 2013.

5. "IFTA: Articles of Agreement."

6. "Executive Order: Establishment of a Coordinator of Federal Support for Recovery and Rebuilding of the Gulf Coast Region." White House, November 1, 2005. Available online: http://georgewbush-whitehouse

.archives.gov/news/releases/2005/11/20051101-8.html. Accessed April 20, 2013.

7. Barry, J. *The Great Influenza: The Story of the Deadliest Pandemic in History* (New York: Penguin Group, 2004).

8. "Media Releases." Novartis Global, 2012. Available online: www.novartis .com/newsroom/media-releases/en/2012/1659272.shtml. Accessed April 20, 2013.

9. Jeffries, C. T. "En Libra: A New Shared Doctrine for Environmental Management," November 3, 1998. Available online: www.azdeq.gov /environ/water/watershed/download/enlibra.pdf. Accessed May 2, 2013.

10. "Drafting the Great Lakes Regional Collaboration Strategy to Restore and Protect the Great Lakes." Great Lakes Regional Collaboration, August 22, 2007. Available online: http://glrc.us/process.html. Accessed April 20, 2013.

11. "About Us." The Streamlined Sales Tax and Use Tax Governing Board, n.d. Available online: www.streamlinedsalestax.org/index.php?page=About-Us. Accessed April 20, 2013.

Chapter 7

1. "Facts about the WRAP." Western Regional Air Partnership, 2009. Available online: www.wrapair.org/facts/index.html. Accessed April 30, 2013.

2. Campbell, C. A. *The One Page Project Manager: Communicate and Manage Any Project with a Single Sheet of Paper* (Hoboken, NJ: Wiley, 2007).

3. "Framework for the Great Lakes Regional Collaboration." Great Lakes Regional Collaboration, n.d. Available online: http://glrc.us/documents /Framework12032004.pdf. Accessed April 20, 2013.

4. "The Global Earth Observation System of Systems (GEOSS): 10-Year Implementation Plan." Group on Earth Observations, February 16, 2005. Available online: www.earthobservations.org/documents/10-Year%20 Implementation%20Plan.pdf. Accessed April 20, 2013.

Chapter 8

1. "IFTA: Articles of Agreement." International Fuel Tax Association, January 2010. Available online: www.iftach.org/manuals/2010/AA/Articles%20of%20 Agreement%20FINAL%20-%20January%202010.pdf. Accessed April 20, 2013.

Chapter 9

1. Vreeman, D. "History, Purpose, and Scope." LOINC from Regenstrief, March 4, 2013. Available online: http://loinc.org/background. Accessed April 20, 2013.

2. "About IHTSDO." International Health Terminology Standards Development Organisation, n.d. Available online: www.ihtsdo.org/about-ihtsdo/. Accessed April 20, 2013. See also: "About HL7." Health Level Seven International, n.d. Available online: www.hl7.org/about/index.cfm. Accessed April 20, 2013.

3. Gabriel, G. "The Evolution of Railroad Standard Gauge." *Discover Live Steam* 34 (2000). Available online: www.discoverlivesteam.com /magazine/34/34.html. Accessed April 19, 2013.

4. "About Us." The Streamlined Sales Tax and Use Tax Governing Board, n.d. Available online: www.streamlinedsalestax.org/index.php?page=About-Us. Accessed April 20, 2013.

Chapter 10

1. Covey, S. R. "Books: The 7 Habits of Highly Effective People. Habit 5: Seek First to Understand, Then to Be Understood." Steven R. Covey, n.d. Available online: www.stephencovey.com/7habits/7habits-habit5.php. Accessed April 20, 2013.

2. Fisher, R., Patton, B., and Ury, W. *Getting to Yes: Negotiating Agreement Without Giving In* (New York: Penguin Books, 1991).

3. General Stanley McChrystal, retired U.S. Army General, personal interview with Governor Mike Leavitt, August 2011. See also McChrystal Group, Shared Consciousness and Purpose," n.d. Available online: www .mcchrystalgroup.com/home. Accessed April 20, 2013. Also: McChrystal, S. *My Share of the Task: A Memoir* (New York: Penguin Group, 2013).

Chapter 11

1. "Ranking #15 Legends Hospitality Management." Food Management, n.d. Available online with registration: http://food-management.com/legends -hospitality-management-2013. Accessed April 20, 2013.

2. "Welcome to Spices Board India." Spices Board India, n.d. Available online: www.indianspices.com/html/spices_board_intro.htm. Accessed April 20, 2013.

3. Rich McKeown, interview with Bill Carlson, former vice president, GHX, June 25, 2012. See also "Company Background." GHX, 2013. Available online: www.ghx.com/about-ghx/company-background.aspx. Accessed May 2, 2013.

4. "About CCHIT." CCHIT, 2013. Available online: www.cchit.org/about. Accessed April 20, 2013.

Appendix: WRAP Charter

1. The Clean Air Act expressly authorizes EPA to treat a tribe in the same manner as a state for the regulation of all air resources within the exterior boundaries of the reservation or other areas within the tribe's jurisdiction without distinguishing among various categories of on-reservation lands. (CAA sections 110 (o), 164(c), 301(d)).

2. Current state and tribal members of the WRAP Board as of 1/1/09 shall automatically be recognized members of the WRAP under this revised Charter, unless otherwise indicated by official letter to the WRAP from that state or tribe.

ACKNOWLEDGMENTS

Finding and working with remarkable allies among our associates has been one of the great opportunities of our collective lives. They have embraced, taught, and mentored us at each venue and stage of our careers. We have developed and refined our alliance-related thinking based on experiences with our colleagues in the private and public sectors. Of particular importance are those in the State of Utah and also at the U.S. Environmental Protection Agency, where formal study and thinking about collaboration took shape and root. We advanced this thinking at the U.S. Department of Health and Human Services and now again with our work partners and clients. We salute them as the primary source of our thinking and for the privilege of working with them in the laboratory of the collaborative experience we have shared. We also appreciate those who participated in interviews, responded to inquiries, and permitted us to write something about the alliances they had both participated in and created. They, along with the previously mentioned colleagues, are the architects and we are merely the organizers of what drives the thought behind *Finding Allies, Building Alliances*.

We appreciate three people who have been instrumental in ensuring that this book became, in the final analysis, a reality: our agent, Scott Hoffman, has been a great advocate for this book; Bruce Wexler, who has patiently helped us with the construction of a final manuscript; and our editor, Karen Murphy, who has demonstrated tremendous insight and an equal amount of patience.

ABOUT THE AUTHORS

Mike Leavitt was elected governor of Utah three times. He then served in the cabinet of President George W. Bush as secretary of HHS and administrator of the EPA. A seasoned diplomat, he has led U.S. delegations to more than fifty countries, conducting negotiations on matters related to health, the environment, and trade. The Chinese government awarded him the China Public Health Award—the first time this award has ever been given to a foreign government official. His fellow governors elected him to serve as chairman of the National Governors Association, the Republican Governors Association, and Western Governors Association.

Before his government service, Leavitt worked for twenty years in the insurance industry. He has since returned to the private sector to found Leavitt Partners, which advises clients in the health care and food safety sectors. He and his wife, Jackie, live in Salt Lake City, Utah. They have five children and eleven grandchildren.

Rich McKeown is cofounder, president, and CEO of Leavitt Partners. He served as chief of staff during Mike Leavitt's terms as governor of Utah, administrator of the EPA, and secretary of HHS. Before working in government, he was an educator, a lawyer, and a mediator. He has worked on and led a wide range of efforts involving technology, education, the environment, health, and international initiatives.

McKeown was born in Washington D.C. and raised in Arlington, Virginia. He and his wife, Barbara, live in Salt Lake City, Utah, and also have five children and eleven grandchildren.

———————

For more information, please visit www.findingallies.com.

INDEX

O

P